Teaching Tools for Every ELA Educator

Author's Purpose Expert

HIGHER-LEVEL THINKING ACTIVITIES FOR GRADES 6-12

➤ *Over 200 story and poem suggestions*
➤ *Questions and exercises which cover state standards*
➤ *Ready-to-use reading and writing lessons*

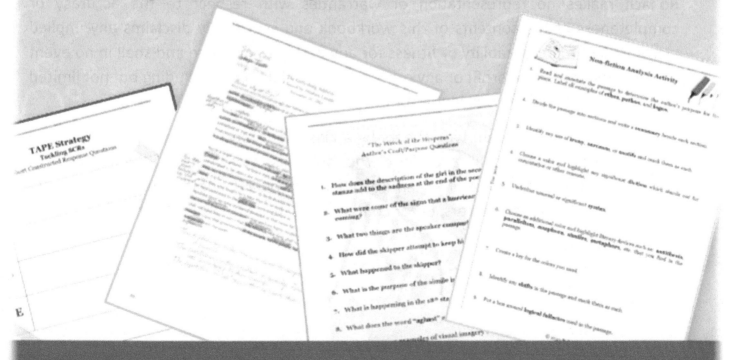

Karen K. Rohach, M.Ed.

Disclaimer Page

Image Credits

No copyright images were used in this book. All images came from the free Shutterstock clipart library or were created or modified using AI systems such as Dall-E2 or Canva.

Copyright

ISBN 979-8386136949

Introduction

No one said teaching was going to be easy, right? Since I started many years ago, it has become so much harder. Believe me, you have my sympathy. The reason I decided to publish this book is because my niece, Ashley, started her first year of teaching this year and I've seen her struggle. New teachers need so much more help than they are getting. Experienced teachers are so busy attending meetings and planning that they don't have time to actually create materials.

The state standards continue to get tougher, so teachers need to keep challenging students by providing higher-level thinking activities. This is the area in which I can be most helpful. My goal in producing this book was to provide the third component of the instructional core, which is academically challenging content. As a result, I have created and gathered useful materials that can be used for both reading and writing.

This collection of materials is divided into three sections. The first section contains activities which can be used to get to know your students and help them get to know each other. The second section contains learning tasks that will help students develop better reading skills. The third section contains learning tasks that will help students develop better writing skills.

At the back of the collection is a bonus section for new teachers. This section contains bits of advice from classroom management to procedures which will help teachers have a better experience in the classroom.

I hope this collection of materials is as beneficial for you as it has been for me. Good luck and best wishes for a great year!

Dedication

I would like to dedicate my book to the following people:

My amazing husband, Timothy Rohach, without whose love, encouragement, and assistance this book would not be possible.

My brilliant father, Robley Davis, who sadly passed away while helping to edit this book after teaching me ethics, responsibility, and the importance of family.

My energetic mother, Ann Davis, whose love and support gave me the courage to make it happen.

Additional Resources

If you find these resources to be helpful and would like activities for the stories and poems listed in this book, you can purchase them at my Teachers Pay Teachers Store *Karen Rohach Author's Purpose Expert.* I have also created many short videos addressing the state standards (TEKS and Common Core.) The videos, as well as contact information, can be found on my website authorspurposeexpert.com. For complete time-saving lessons for teachers that can be used with or without the provided scripts, checkout my other books on Amazon.

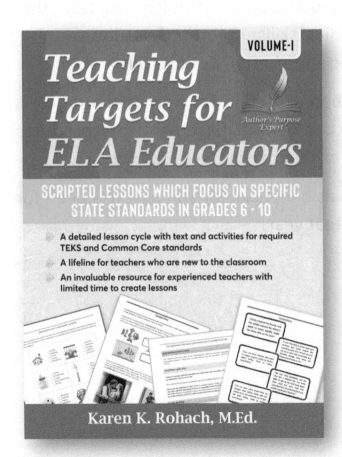

Table of Contents

SECTION ONE

ICE BREAKERS

"Go out into the world today and love the people you meet. Let your presence light new light in the hearts of others."

Mother Theresa

 # Classroom Bingo

Find a different person to sign their name in each box. When each box has been filled, call out "Bingo"!

I have a cat.	I was born in January.	I play soccer.	I like pepperoni pizza.
My shoes have no laces.	I have curly hair.	I have two younger siblings.	I was at a different school last year.
I have traveled on an airplane.	I was not born in Texas.	I wear glasses.	I write with my left hand.
I know the principal's name.	I speak two languages.	My first name starts with a J.	My favorite color is purple.
I have read a whole book with chapters.	I have a summer birthday.	There are more than 4 kids in my family.	I like vegetables.

Find Someone in This Class Who...

1. _____ has brown eyes.

2. _____ has a dog.

3. _____ likes math.

4. _____ wears glasses.

5. _____ is left-handed.

6. _____ likes pepperoni pizza.

7. _____ was born in August.

8. _____ likes to read.

9. _____ can count to ten in Spanish.

10. _____ has traveled on an airplane.

11. _____ likes to sing.

12. _____ is a good artist.

13. _____ has been on a boat.

14. _____ has a younger sister.

15. _____ has an older brother.

16. _____ has a cat.

17. _____ was born in Texas.

18. _____ likes to cook.

19. _____ doesn't like seafood.

20. _____ knows the principal's name.

Would You Rather Questions

Ask students questions and have them answer by raising their hands, moving to one side of the room, or using erasable whiteboards. Discuss with students why they answered as they did.

Throughout the year, you can ask questions relating to content.

- Would you rather be extremely tall or extremely short?

- Would you rather have a lot of friends or be really smart?

- Would you rather be trapped in a room with 30 screaming babies or one hungry alligator?

- Would you rather be a famous actor or a famous singer?

- Would you rather be very rich or very famous?

- Would you rather have no teeth or no hair?

- Would you rather lose your sense of sight or lose your sense of hearing?

- Would you rather take a bath in ice cubes or take a bath in tomato soup?

- Would you rather ride a bike on ice or roller skate down a ramp with sand?

- Would you rather play indoors or outdoors?

- Would you rather see a firework display or a circus performance?

- Would you rather go to an amusement park or a water park?

- Would you rather everything in your house be one color or every single wall and door a different color?

- Would you rather visit the international space station for a week or stay in an underwater hotel for a week?

- Would you rather eat cake or pie?

D Ice Breakers

Have the students roll the die and answer the questions attached.

 If you could go anywhere in the world, where would you go?

 If you were stranded on a desert island, what three things would you want to have with you?

 If you could eat only one food for the rest of your life, what would it be?

 If you won a million dollars, what is the first thing you would buy?

 If you could spend the day with one famous person, who would it be?

 If you found a magic lantern and a genie gave you three wishes, what would you wish for?

Color-Coded Q & A

Write the colors and questions listed below on the board for students to see. Use colored toothpicks, M&Ms, popsicle sticks, etc. and have students choose a color for their response to the following questions:

Red: What is one of your favorite things you did this summer?

Blue: If you could have a superpower, what would it be?

Green: If you could be any animal, what would it be and why?

Purple: What is something you can't live without and why?

Yellow: If you could go anywhere in the world, where would you go and what would you do?

Orange: What is a talent you have and when did you first learn you were good at it?

 **Form a Line**

Have students organize themselves and line up in a certain order. You can set a time limit to make it more challenging. Here are some suggestions:

- Youngest to oldest (by birthday)

- Oldest to youngest (by birthday)

- Tallest to shortest

- Shortest to tallest

- Alphabetical order by first name

- Alphabetical order by last name

- Length of hair

- Color of hair (darkest to lightest)

Six Word Story

Have students explain what they did over the summer using only six words, writing the statement as a complete sentence on a piece of paper. Then, have students exchange papers with a classmate and have the classmate add a comment comprised of only six words. You may choose to rotate the papers to adjust the length of the story to your preference.

Speed Rating

Make a seating chart with all of the students in the class. Use boxes to represent desks and write each student's name in a box.

Have students in every other desk stand up and then give them the directions on how they will rotate while the other students will remain seated during the whole activity. Tell them to sit down and give them 1 minute and 30 seconds to ask the person they are sitting next to as many questions as they can while taking notes. When the time expires, have the stationary person ask the rotating person as many questions as they can for the next 1 minute and 30 seconds while taking notes. After that time, have the students rotate. Continue the same pattern until everyone has interviewed all of the students in the classroom.

Have students sit in their assigned seats and hand them a blank seating chart. Tell students to fill in as much information as they can on the seating chart about each student.

Pick two random students to tell the class as much information as they can about each other. Continue calling on students until everyone has spoken.

Jenga Quest

You will probably need several Jenga (or similar) games for this activity. Take the tiles from a Jenga game and write questions on them. These questions might include the following:

- What is your favorite subject?

- What is your favorite food?

- If you could go anywhere in the world, where would you go?

- Who is your best friend and how long have you been friends with them?

- How do you most like to spend your free time?

Put students into small groups with a Jenga tower and have them take turns drawing tiles and answering the questions on the tiles. Choose one student in each group to keep score of how many questions each person in their group answers. The student who has the most points when the tower topples wins.

Stand Up

Stand at the front of the room and ask students to stand up next to their desk if they can answer yes to the question. Have them sit down between the questions.

- Your favorite flavor of ice cream is vanilla.
- You have a dog.
- You have traveled out of the country.
- Your favorite color is purple.
- You went to a water park this summer.
- You like pineapple on your pizza.
- You have watched the entire series of *Stranger Things*.
- You have created a power point presentation.
- You are good at math.
- You know how to play an instrument.
- You like to play sports.
- You have been to the beach.
- You know what you want to do after you graduate.
- You have lived in the same place all of your life.
- You are good at drawing.
- You know how to write in cursive.

You can do a variation of this game by drawing a line down the center of the room and having one side for yes and the other side for no. Have students move to the appropriate side after each question.

Problem Solving Activity

Complete the following activity as a group with each member writing on his/her own paper.

A boy named Josh, who is the same age as the members in your group, has been stranded on a deserted island. Discuss the four most important qualities and abilities he would need in order to survive the situation. Provide a reason for each of the abilities that you chose.

Abilities	Reasons

Make a list of the five most important/useful objects to have when stranded on a deserted island with #1 being the most important:

1.

2.

3.

4.

5.

Individual Sinking Ship Activity

The Situation

After seven days of sailing in horrible weather, the ship on which you are a passenger is about to sink somewhere in the Pacific Ocean. The captain has lost all contact with the outside world, but he hopes that the ship is not far from some uninhabited Pacific Islands.

The captain informs you that the ship will go down within a few minutes. He orders you to wake up five (<u>only five</u>) of the sleeping passengers, because the lifeboat, unfortunately, only has room for five out of the ten passengers in addition to you and the captain. He hands you the passenger list and tells you to choose five.

Passenger List

Stacey (Age 30) – Social worker, member of her church choir, former chef

Twan (Age 53) – Very skillful nurse from Vietnam, racist and spiteful

Ashley (Age 18) – Swedish nerd, speaks 12 languages fluently and never keeps her mouth shut, sings Taylor Swift songs when nobody will talk to her

Roderick (Age 27) – Very skillful football player on the Texans, discreet and loyal

John (Age 44) – Police officer and ex-military specialist, guilty of domestic violence

Marcus (Age 38) – Jack-of-all-trades and a master of survival, suspected of having connections to Al Qaida

Nelson Mandela (Age 95) – Winner of the Nobel Peace Prize and highly respected former head of state

Marcella (Age 20) – Supermodel, millionaire, amazingly pretty, but amazingly stupid

Zeke (Age 9) – Smart, cheerful, and always helpful, tends to make everyone happy with his presence

Rosa (Age 35) – Zeke's mother and only living relative, has a terminal illness and only three months to live

The Survivors

Write the names of the people who get to board the lifeboat and the reason you chose each:

1._____

_____

2._____

_____

3._____

_____

4._____

_____

5._____

_____

Individual Writing Activities

Choose from one of the following writing activities:

1. Write a series of journal entries starting with two days before the ship goes down and three days after.

2. Write a letter to a loved one knowing that you may never see them again.

3. Write a magazine article describing your time on a Pacific Island and how you were saved.

4. Write a poem about your experience with the shipwreck.

5. Write the first chapter of your book about the whole experience.

SECTION TWO

READING

"I have a passion for teaching kids to become readers, to become comfortable with a book, not daunted. Books shouldn't be daunting, they should be funny, exciting, and wonderful; and learning to be a reader gives a terrific advantage."

Roald Dahl

Comprehensive List of Short Stories for Grades 6 - 12
With Summaries, Themes, and Pairing Suggestions

2BR02B
Kurt Vonnegut

Summary: This story occurs in a dystopian society in which a person has to die in order for a newborn to live. A young father is faced with an impossible choice when his triplets are born.

Theme: People will do crazy and unreasonable things to protect the ones they love. Death is a natural process that should not be controlled.

A Burlesque Biography
Mark Twain

Summary: Mark Twain gives a humorous account of his ancestors.

Theme: Everyone's ancestry is unique.

A Dead Woman's Secret
Guy de Maupassant

Summary: Two adults are at their mother's death bed and find out a secret about her.

Theme: People are not always who we think they are.

A Dog's Tale
Mark Twain

Summary: A dog tells the story of his life through his own eyes.

Theme: It is wrong to sacrifice animals for the benefit of man.

A Respectable Woman
Kate Chopin

Summary: This is a typical Chopin story about a woman's repression. After a period of self-reflection, she decides whether or not to have an affair with her husband's visiting friend.

Theme: People aren't always as they seem. No one is perfect. This story would pair well with **The Story of an Hour.**

A Retrieved Reformation
O. Henry

Summary: A career criminal is chased by a lawman as he attempts to straighten out his life.

Theme: Love can reform anyone.

A Sound of Thunder
Ray Bradbury

Summary: A man goes back in time through a machine, accidentally steps on a butterfly, and changes the present as a result.

Theme: Everything in life has a purpose and there is a causal connection for all events. There are things interlinked to a degree that we cannot see, so to disrupt one element could be catastrophic.

A Visit of Charity
Eudora Welty

Summary: A Campfire girl goes to visit a nursing home to fulfill requirements and receive bonus points.

Theme: Charity is wrong if it is done for the wrong reason.

A Worn Path
Eudora Welty

Summary: An old woman makes an arduous journey through the dead of winter and encounters many obstacles.

Theme: The author explores the theme of immortality in a number of ways in the short story, including the cycles of nature, imagery, and the main character's name.

After Twenty Years
O. Henry

Summary: Two friends honor their pact to meet at a certain spot twenty years later. The results are unexpected.

Theme: Love can reform anyone. Honor is more important than friendship.

All Summer in a Day
Ray Bradbury

Summary: A girl is having trouble adjusting to her life on Venus where the sun only comes out for one day every seven years. As she awaits her opportunity to see the sun, something unexpected happens.

Theme: Jealousy can cause people to do bad things.

An Occurrence at Owl Creek Bridge
Ambrose Bierce

Summary: A soldier is being hung on a bridge when the rope breaks and he has a hazardous trip back to his home. He suddenly wakes up and realizes that he has been day-dreaming in the instant before he dies.

Theme: The line between dreams and reality is thin. There is no romance or glory in war.

Average Waves in Unprotected Waters
Anne Tyler

Summary: A single mother must make the most difficult decision in her life.

Theme: No matter how strong we are and how hard we try, sometimes we have to give up and admit defeat.

Barney
Will Stanton

Summary: A man conducts an intelligence experiment on a mouse and the experiment backfires.

Theme: Man should never interfere or alter God's creations.

Blue Ain't No Mockin Bird
Toni Cade Bambara

Summary: A reporter tries to manipulate a family and use them as a model for others, but the family doesn't want any part of it.

Theme: It is wrong to exploit the misfortunes of others.

Calling the Shots
Karen Dionne

Summary: A man decides to abandon his pregnant girlfriend due to his extreme dislike of her mother, and this leads to dire consequences.

Theme: You reap what you sow. What goes around comes around.

Catch the Moon
Judith Ortiz Cofer

Summary: A juvenile delinquent returns to work at his father's car junkyard when he develops feelings for a girl he meets there. She helps him to work through the pain of his mother's death.

Theme: The power of love can change people.

Cemetery Path
Leonard Q. Ross

Summary: A man known as a coward in the town is challenged to walk across the cemetery at night.

Theme: If we give in to our fears, they will destroy us.

Charles
Shirley Jackson

Summary: A young boy gives daily reports to his parents about a bad boy at school only for them to find out that their son isn't as innocent as he seems.

Theme: Children are often not as innocent as they are perceived by their parents.

Dark They Were and Golden-Eyed
Ray Bradbury

Summary: When a family moves to a new colony on Mars, the father begins to have concerns about what is happening to them.

Theme: The grass is not always greener on the other side of the fence.

Death by Scrabble
Charlie Fish

Summary: A man and his wife are playing scrabble during a summer heatwave and the longer he plays, the more he wants to kill her.

Theme: Things don't always go as expected. This is a **macabre/humorous** story that is good to teach for **irony**. It would pair well with **Ruthless.**

Edward Mills and George Benton:
A Tale by Mark Twain

Summary: This is a story of two cousins who are very opposite in morals and ambition. It also serves as a message about society.

Theme: We should praise, celebrate, and reward those in our society who are not a burden rather than rewarding those who continually make mistakes or choose not to follow the laws. This story would pair well with Twain's stories **The Story of the Bad Little Boy** and **The Story of the Good Little Boy.**

Eleven
Sandra Cisneros

Summary: A young girl describes how her teacher humiliates her on her eleventh birthday.

Theme: No matter how old you are, there are moments in life when you feel like a child. Sometimes people who are in authority and the ones you are supposed to count on are the ones who let you down. This story would pair well with **White Lies.**

Examination Day
Henry Slesar

Summary: This is a futuristic story about a boy who is forced to take a government test on his twelfth birthday to determine if he is too smart to continue living.

Theme: This story emphasizes the danger of fear, suppression, control, freedom and expression. This story would pair well with **Harrison Bergeron.**

Fish Cheeks
Amy Tan

Summary: A girl is mortified about the cultural meal that her mother serves to the minister and his son on whom she has a crush. She later learns of her mother's motives.

Theme: You should never be ashamed of your family or culture, because that is your foundation.

From Here to Sargasso
Andrew S. Williams

Summary: A mother and daughter are walking on the beach and see the unique site of baby turtles making their way to the sea.

Theme: The young must make their own way in life. Home is wherever a person feels accepted.

Garden of Statues
Justin Richards

Summary: This story is a sort of parable about a man who is extremely jealous of his neighbor's garden, but the jealousy leads to his downfall.

Theme: If you aren't content with what you have, you may lose everything.

Gilray's Flower Pot
J.M. Barrie

Summary: A man agrees to take responsibility for another man's plant but later makes excuses as to why it died.

Theme: People should take responsibility for their own actions.

Harrison Bergeron
Kurt Vonnegut, Jr.

Summary: This is a futuristic story about a dystopian society that does not allow anyone to have exceptions to what is average. One young man attempts to question and defy authority.

Theme: This story highlights the dangers of focusing on artificial equality rather than celebrating differences. This story pairs well with **Examination Day.**

Hey, You Down There
Harold Rolseth

Summary: An abusive husband discovers a deep hole on his land which leads to a bizarre civilization. His wife communicates with the civilization which leads to an interesting chain of events.

Theme: What goes around comes around. You reap what you sow. This would pair well with **Lamb to the Slaughter.**

Home
Gwendolyn Brooks

Summary: Mama, Helen, and Maud Martha wait for Papa to get home from the loan company to find out if he has gotten an extension on the house loan. They try to make themselves feel better by talking about how much they dislike the house and how much better they will live if they don't get the extension. The story ends with them all happy due to the fact that Papa got the extension.

Theme: Sometimes we don't appreciate things until we are about to lose them.

Identities
W.D. Valgardson

Summary: A man makes the mistake of roaming into the wrong part of town, and this leads to a serious misunderstanding.

Theme: People should not be identified according to perceptions because it can lead to bad circumstances.

In Memoriam
Ray Bradbury

Summary: A father grieves the loss of his son due to war and attempts to find a way to heal.

Theme: Loved ones who have died are always with us. Sometimes it is necessary to accept things and move on.

Jeff Peters as a Personal Magnet
O. Henry

Summary: A traveling conman runs into an old acquaintance and attempts to con the Mayor.

Theme: It isn't wise to con a conman.

Just in Time for Spring
Ellis Weiner

Summary: This is a **satiric** piece about the wonders of going outside which targets young people who stay on their phones and computers.

Theme: Appreciate nature and its beauty rather than wasting your life inside with technology.

Lamb to the Slaughter
Roald Dahl

Summary: A woman tries to be a perfect wife for her husband but is devastated when he tells her he is leaving her. Her actions as a result serve as a surprising twist to the reader.

Theme: Hell hath no fury like a woman scorned.

Let's Play Poison
Ray Bradbury

Summary: This story is about a grumpy teacher who has issues with a game that his students play and what happens as a result.

Theme: If you seek trouble, trouble will find you. Children are not as innocent as they seem. This would pair well with **Ruthless.**

Love is a Fallacy
Max Shulman

Summary: A young man attempts to teach a girl who he considers ignorant but is attracted to only to have her use the knowledge against him.

Theme: Treat others as you would have them treat you.

Luck
Mark Twain

Summary: This is a satirical story about a military man who rises through the ranks due to luck in spite of his ignorance.

Theme: People in our society are often praised or idolized based on expectations of them rather than their actual talent and abilities.

Marigolds
Eugenia W. Collier

Summary: During the Depression, an old woman surrounds her dilapidated house with beautiful marigolds to the dismay of a girl and her friends.

Theme: There can be beauty in decay, and we should appreciate it rather than resent it. This pairs well with the Mrs. Dubose and Jem incident in *To Kill a Mockingbird*.

Men are Different
Alan Bloch

Summary: A robot describes his encounter and understanding of men.

Theme: Making assumptions can cause serious issues.

This pairs well with the story **Zoo.**

Moon-Face
Jack London

Summary: The speaker describes the actions he is willing to go through due to his hatred of another man.

Theme: Jealousy can bring out the worst in people.

My First Free Summer
Julia Alvarez

Summary: A young girl from the Dominican Republic spends every summer learning English, but the lessons pay off with her family's arrival in the United States.

Theme: Anything is possible with determination and a will to make it happen.

My Kid's Dog
Ron Hansen

Summary: This is a **humorous** story about a man who hates the family dog and his attempts to dispose of it after it dies.

Theme: No matter how irritating or unpleasant a family member may be, they are still an inseparable part of the family that brings harmony and joy.

Only Daughter
Sandra Cisneros

Summary: A daughter wants the approval of her father early in her career.

Theme: Parents should be aware of the role they play in their children's futures.

Possessions
John Smolens

Summary: A man is dealing with the death of his wife and the things that represent her.

Theme: Even when a loved one dies, a part of them is always with us.

Rain, Rain, Go Away
Isaac Asimov

Summary: This is a story about a family who is extremely afraid of water. The story has a surprise ending when the reader discovers that they are made of sugar.

Theme: There are some things that we can't control. Nosey neighbors should keep to themselves.

Raymond's Run
Toni Cade Bambara

Summary: A girl wants to be the best at running, her only talent, so she trains for races by running all the time. Her mentally disabled brother follows her everywhere. During a race, the girl discovers that her brother is a better runner than she is, so she decides to start training him to be the best.

Theme: You have to find your own identity in order to best aid others.

Ruthless
William de Mille

Summary: An angry man puts poison in his liquor to kill whoever is stealing it at his lake house during the off season. This is a good story to teach **irony**.

Theme: Revenge can lead to awful consequences. This would pair well with **Death by Scrabble.**

Salvation
Langston Hughes

Summary: A boy loses his faith in God due to the pressure put on him at his aunt's church revival. This is a good story for **irony**.

Theme: Sometimes the best intentions have the worst outcomes.

Segregationist
Isaac Asimov

Summary: In a world where man and robot work together, one man has to decides the type of surgery he wants.

Theme: The line between man and robot is becoming more and more thin.

This story would pair well with **Men are Different.**

Seventh Grade
Gary Soto

Summary: A seventh grade boy tries to impress a girl he has a crush on with the help of his French teacher.

Theme: People will go to any lengths to impress those they care about.

Skin
Roald Dahl

Summary: An old man enters an art gallery when he notices that the art is from the same man who tattooed his back years ago with a picture of his wife. The man attempts to make money by selling himself for the artwork.

Theme: People will sometimes do anything when they are desperate for money.

Snow
Julia Alvarez

Summary: A young immigrant girl has been experiencing preparing for the Cuban Missile Crisis at school when she sees snow for the first time.

Theme: It is easy for people to get caught up in the problems of society and not notice the important things in life.

Stop the Sun
Gary Paulsen

Summary: A young man is embarrassed by his father's actions until he realizes what happened to his father during the war.

Theme: Don't judge others unless you have walked in their shoes.

Sunday in the Park
Bel Kaufman

Summary: A woman with her young son has an incident in the park which ends up making her question her husband and herself.

Theme: People shouldn't let the misguided actions of others control their thoughts and feelings. The norms and expectations of society aren't always right.

Test
Theodore L. Thomas

Summary: This is a futuristic story about a young man who is driving with his mother when he has a terrible accident. He realizes that he is actually taking his driver's test and the accident isn't real.

Theme: The government shouldn't determine what's in a person's conscience. This story would pair well with **Examination Day.**

Thank You, Ma'am
Langston Hughes

Summary: A boy tries to steal the purse of an old lady when she grabs him and takes him to her home. She feeds him, shows him respect, and gives him money in hopes that it will make an impression on him.

Theme: Grace and second chances can often change a person.

The Awful Fate of Melpomenus Jones
Stephen Leacock

Summary: A young man's fear of being rude causes his demise.

Theme: Confusion and fear is a powerful motivation that can lead people to make unimaginable decisions.

The Black Cat
Edgar Allan Poe

Summary: A man kills his wife and conceals her body but is caught due to a cat.

Theme: It is very difficult to escape justice. The truth usually wins out. This story would pair well with **The Cask of Amontillado.**

The Cask of Amontillado
Edgar Allan Poe

Summary: A man seeks revenge on his former friend by getting him drunk and burying him alive.

Theme: Treat others the way you want to be treated. This story would pair well with **The Black Cat.**

The Chaser
John Collier

Summary: A young man goes to see a chemist to get a love potion so that the girl he is infatuated with will fall completely in love with him. The apothecary sells him the potion for one dollar knowing that someday he will return for the antidote which sells for $5000.

Theme: Be careful what you wish for. The grass is not always greener on the other side of the fence. This is a good story to teach **irony**. This would pair well with **Was It a Dream?**

The Continuity of Parks
Julio Cortazar

Summary: This story is about a man who has a cheating wife. The story ends with an interesting twist.

Theme: Things aren't always as we expect.

The Cricket on the Hearth
Ray Bradbury

Summary: This story is about a couple who find out that their house is bugged by the government and the surprising effect it has on their marriage.

Theme: No matter how much people attempt to make changes in their lives, they usually go back to what they're most comfortable with.

The Dinner Party
Mona Gardner

Summary: A woman is giving a dinner party in India when one of the guests realize that a cobra is in the room.

Theme: We must take control or make the most of any situation no matter how bad it is.

The Elevator
William Sleator

Summary: A boy continues to have a terrifying encounter in the building elevator.

Theme: Trust your instinct.

The Escape
J.B. Stamper

Summary: A prisoner believes he has found a way to escape only to discover his greatest fear realized.

Theme: No matter how hard you try, your sins will catch up with you.

The Eyes Have It
Philip K. Dick

Summary: This is a **humorous** story about a man who takes **idioms** literally while reading a story leading him to believe that there are aliens among us.

Theme: It is not always a good idea to take things literally.

The Falling Girl
Dino Buzzati

Summary: This is a story about a girl who is falling from a building and the sights and sounds she experiences on her way down.

Theme: There is a vast difference between the rich and the poor in our society. Life goes on.

The Far and the Near
Thomas Wolfe

Summary: A retiring railroad engineer who has passed by the same house and women for over twenty years makes an attempt to meet the women. The result of meeting them is not as he had expected.

Theme: Perception is reality but is often far from the truth.

The Flowers
Alice Walker

Summary: A young girl is playing in the woods and admiring the beautiful flowers when she comes across a dead body.

Theme: This story shows the contrast between the beauty of innocence and the ugliness of reality.

The Fly
Katherine Mansfield

Summary: A businessman reflects on the life of his son who was killed in the war when he sees a fly struggling to get out of his inkpot.

Theme: Life is fragile and can easily be taken by the actions of others.

The Flying Machine
Ray Bradbury

Summary: This story takes place in 400 A.D. China. It is about a man who invents a flying machine and what happens as a result.

Theme: Sometimes it is necessary to sacrifice beauty and creativity for the safety of others. Inventions can be used for both good and evil. This story would pair well with **Barney.**

The Friday Everything Changed
Anne Hart

Summary: A group of girls are tired of being treated as unequal to the boys, and with the help of their teacher make some necessary changes.

Theme: We should never stop fighting for the things we believe to be right.

The Fun They Had
Isaac Asimov

Summary: This is a futuristic story about two kids who are currently taught by computers but find a book describing how schools used to look.

Theme: If we keep relying on technology, we may lose the importance of social interaction. This story could lead to a good discussion about how the Coronavirus has affected us. This story would pair well with **There Will Come Soft Rains.**

The Gift of the Magi
O Henry

Summary: A young, poor couple sacrifice their most treasured items to buy each other a gift for Christmas but end up not needing the gifts they received due to their sacrifice. This story is a great example of **irony**. This story would serve as a good contrast to **The Lady or the Tiger**.

Theme: True love means being willing to sacrifice our most precious possessions.

The Golden Kite, the Silver Wind
Ray Bradbury

Summary: Two towns begin to have a dispute which leads to the continuing rebuilding of both of their city walls and the slow deterioration of the cities.

Theme: War isn't good for anyone.

The Green Door
O. Henry

Summary: A man decides to take a chance and enter through a mysterious door only to find out later it wasn't what he thought it was.

Theme: Sometimes it is necessary to take risks in life to find the best things. Nothing ventured, nothing gained.

The Hanging Stanger
Philip Dick

Summary: This is a science fiction story about a man who is confused when strange things start happening around him and people are reacting unexpectedly.

Theme: Be aware of others attempting to take control of your society and sense of safety. This story would pair well with **Dark They Were and Golden-Eyed.**

The Interlopers
Saki

Summary: Two men from feuding families meet in a forest and are trapped together under a fallen tree. They agree to stop the feud and make amends when a pack of wolves shows up.

Theme: Live life to the fullest because you never know when it will end. The force of nature is more powerful than the petty feuds of men.

The Invalid's Story
Mark Twain

Summary: This is a **humorous** story about a man who has to escort his friend's body across the country on a train. Someone unknowingly puts cheese in the coffin and the reaction is hilarious.

Theme: Don't make assumptions when you don't know the facts.

The Lady or the Tiger
Frank R. Stockton

Summary: This story is about a ruthless king whose daughter falls in love with a man of lower status. The king punishes the couple by forcing the man to choose between two doors containing a beautiful lady which he must marry or a tiger which will kill him.

Theme: If you truly love someone, it is better to let them go. This story would serve as a good contrast to **The Gift of the Magi**.

The Lake
Ray Bradbury

Summary: This story is about a boy who experiences a tragic loss. He moves on but is faced with it again when he returns to his hometown as a newlywed.

Theme: We can't replace those who are most important in our lives. We should remember the past but not hold on to it.

The Landlady
Roald Dahl

Summary: A young man on a business trip makes a life-changing decision.

Theme: You can't judge a book by its cover.

The Last of Her Sons
Alden Nowlan

Summary: A mother has hopes for her youngest son after the others have followed their father's footsteps into alcoholism and abuse.

Theme: No matter how hard a person tries to change destiny, sometimes it is impossible.

The Last Leaf
O. Henry

Summary: A heartfelt story about an old man who is willing to risk his life for a young lady who lives nearby.

Theme: A true friend is willing to make sacrifices to help a friend in need. A person should never give up hope no matter what the circumstance.

The Leopard Man's Story
Jack London

Summary: A circus man describes a fascinating story of revenge.

Theme: Man should respect nature and not take its wildness for granted.

The Lottery Ticket
Anton P. Chekhov

Summary: A man and his wife find out that they are extremely close to winning the lottery and start imagining how they will spend the money.

Theme: Greed and the desire for money can corrupt anyone.

The Man in the Well
Ira Sher

Summary: A group of children come across a man trapped in a well and must decide what to do.

Theme: It is easier to go along with the crowd rather than doing what is right.

The Masque of the Red Death
Edgar Allan Poe

Summary: A prince tries to cheat death by locking himself and others in his castle while a plague is going on.

Theme: Death is inescapable. This story is a good way to teach **allegory.**

The Monkey's Paw
W.W. Jacobs

Summary: A family receives a monkey's paw which grants them three wishes. The wishes lead to a terrible outcome.

Theme: Be satisfied with what you have. Be careful what you wish for. This story would pair well with **The Third Wish.**

The Mouse
Saki

Summary: A young man's upbringing causes him to be extremely uncomfortable in an awkward situation with a young lady.

Theme: The sheltering effects of wealth and privilege can foster irritability and weakness rather than happiness.

The Most Dangerous Game
Richard Connell

Summary: A man accidentally ends up on a nearly deserted island to find out the man who lives on the island hunts humans for sport. He is hunted by the man for three days but ends up killing the hunter in the end.

Theme: Man is unique because he has the ability to reason. This is what makes him so dangerous.

The Moustache
Robert Cormier

Summary: A young man visits his grandmother in a nursing home when he is mistaken by her as her husband. This leads to him finding out things about his grandparents that he would rather not know.

Theme: Childhood only lasts for a short period of time, so we should enjoy it rather than trying to grow up too fast.

The Necklace
Guy de Maupassant

Summary: A poor woman and her husband are invited to a ball, so she borrows a necklace from a wealthy acquaintance. She accidentally loses the necklace and spends ten years and the prime of her youth doing hard labor to earn the money to pay for the necklace. This is a good story to teach **irony**.

Theme: Be satisfied with who you are and what you have.

The Nice People
Henry Cuyler Bunner

Summary: While on vacation, a couple doubts the validity of a young couple's stories.

Theme: People shouldn't judge or make assumptions about others because you never know what they're going through.

The Night the Ghost Got In
James Thurber

Summary: This is a humorous story about a family who experience a strange noise in the night and the craziness that ensues.

Theme: Just because people are old doesn't mean they are senile.

The Party
Pam Munoz Ryan

Summary: A girl is not invited to a popular girl's party until one of the other girls is unable to come. The girl must then decide whether or not to go to the party knowing that she wasn't the initial choice.

Theme: People should accept themselves the way they are rather than trying to please others. This story pairs well with **The Stolen Party.**

The Pedestrian
Ray Bradbury

Summary: This is a futuristic story about a man who walks at night so that people won't question his sanity due to the fact that he prefers to be outdoors rather than inside using technology.

Theme: Too much technology can warp a society's perceptions so much that simple, natural activities, such as taking a walk, are seen as signs of insanity. This story will pair well with the short stories, **"The Story of an Hour"** or **"There Will Come Soft Rains."**

The Pit and the Pendulum
Edgar Allan Poe

Summary: A soldier during the Spanish Inquisition is captured and sentenced to death by being placed in a room with a large pendulum and a pit in the center. He has to choose between being killed from the pendulum or dying in the pit. At the last minute he is saved.

Theme: No matter how dire the circumstances, the will to live eventually takes over.

The Scholarship Jacket
Martha Salinas

Summary: A school board decides to start charging money for the school jacket to prevent a girl from being able to obtain one. Her grandfather teaches her a valuable lesson.

Theme: Hard work pays off. People shouldn't be afraid to speak up if they know something isn't right.

The Schoolmistress
Anton Chekhov

Summary: A schoolteacher in Russia reflects on her miserable life while taking a journey into town to get her salary and supplies.

Theme: You can choose to accept your condition in life or try to change it.

The Secret Life of Walter Mitty
James Thurber

Summary: A man who is bored with his mundane life creates fantasies in order to make himself feel better.

Theme: Sometimes it is easier to pretend than face the realities of life.

The Singing Lesson
Katherine Mansfield

Summary: In the 1920s, a teacher expresses her feelings about a broken engagement through the music she teaches her students.

Theme: It is difficult for most people to hide their feelings when something tragic happens, but we shouldn't take it out on those around us.

The Sniper
Liam O'Flaherty

Summary: A sniper on a rooftop during the Irish Civil War shoots at his enemies, later to find out that he has killed his brother. This is a good story for **irony**.

Theme: War changes everyone and can divide families.

The Stolen Party
Liliana Heker

Summary: A girl is invited to a party for the daughter of her mother's employer and misunderstands the reason that she has been invited.

Theme: People are too often judged for what they have rather than who they are.

The Storm
McKnight Malmar

Summary: As a woman eagerly waits for her husband during a terrible storm, she encounters terrifying events.

Theme: People should not settle for a life in which they are not happy.

The Story of an Hour
Kate Chopin

Summary: A young woman discovers that her husband has been killed in an accident, and she begins to realize that she will finally be free from the constraints of society. When she sees her husband walk through the door due to a mistake in the report, she instantly dies. This is a great example of **irony**.

Theme: Living without independence is not really living. This story would pair well with **A Respectable Woman.**

The Story of the Bad Little Boy
Mark Twain

Summary: This story is about a boy who is bad throughout his entire life and what happens to him as a result.

Theme: The reality of life is often depressing, and people don't always get what they deserve. This story pairs well with **The Story of the Good Little Boy** and **Edward Mills and George Benton: A Tale by Mark Twain.**

The Story of the Good Little Boy
Mark Twain

Summary: This story is about a boy who is good throughout his whole life and what happens to him as a result.

Theme: If you're not helping people for the right reasons, you shouldn't be helping them at all. This story pairs well with **The Story of the Bad Little Boy** and **Edward Mills and George Benton: A Tale by Mark Twain.**

The Tell-Tale Heart
Edgar Allan Poe

Summary: A man unjustly kills an old man who is living with him and begins to go crazy, thinking he hears the old man's heart beating.

Theme: Fear can shape how we perceive things and how we react. Guilt is a powerful motivator.

The Terrible Old Man
H.P. Lovecraft

Summary: Three criminals make an elaborate plan to rob an old man.

Theme: Don't judge a book by its cover.

The Third Wish
Joan Aiken

Summary: A man gets three wishes when he rescues a swan, so he wishes for a beautiful wife. The wife is perfect but becomes unhappy because she is actually a swan, so he uses the second wish to turn her back into a swan. He lives the rest of his days content with his swan wife nearby. He dies happily without ever using his last wish.

Theme: If you love something, you should set it free. This story would pair well with **The Monkey's Paw.**

The Treasure in the Forest
H.G. Wells

Summary: Two criminals acquire a treasure map through nefarious means, but karma ends up changing their plans.

Theme: The path of greed and crime is always destructive.

The Veldt
Ray Bradbury

Summary: This is a science fiction story about parents who overindulge their children and what happens as a result.

Theme: Technology can be good or evil depending on who is using it.

The Weapon
Fredric Brown

Summary: A man tries to stop another man from creating a weapon of mass destruction by any means necessary.

Theme: Sometimes it is easier to see the fault in others than it is to see the fault in ourselves.

The Wife's Story
Ursula K. Leguin

Summary: A woman is happily married until her husband starts acting strangely. A surprising twist is revealed in the end.

Theme: Perception is reality. What is normal for some is terrifying for others.

The Wish
Roald Dahl

Summary: A little boy wants a puppy for his birthday, so he uses his imagination to make a deal.

Theme: It is important for kids to use their imaginations, and it is important to overcome our fears.

The Years of My Birth
Louise Erdrich

Summary: A child with a birth defect is rejected by her mother until her mother contacts her as an adult requesting help to save her brother.

Theme: You reap what you sow. What goes around comes around.

There Will Come Soft Rains
Ray Bradbury

Summary: This is a futuristic story about a house that survives a nuclear attack and how the technology continues even though the humans have perished.

Theme: War can lead to the end of humanity while technology is powerful enough to live without humans. This story would pair well with **The Fun They Had.**

They're Made Out of Meat
Terry Bisson

Summary: Aliens discover an unusual planet in which the beings are made out of meat.

Theme: It is wrong to judge other people and consider yourself to be better than others. This story would pair well with **Hey, You Down There.**

Three Questions
Leo Tolstoy

Summary: A king searches for the answers to life's most important questions and finds them by accident.

Theme: The most important time is now, the most important person is whoever you are with, and the most important thing is help the person you are with.

Time Enough at Last
Lynn Venable

Summary: This story is about a man who is the only survivor when a war causes the annihilation of the world. This allows him to finally have the time to read, which is his favorite thing to do.

Theme: Be careful what you wish for, because it may not be worth the consequences. Man is destined to destroy himself. There is a famous "Twilight Zone" episode which covers this story.

Two Friends
Guy de Maupassant

Summary: Two old friends take a risky fishing trip during wartime and are faced with a decision of loyalty.

Theme: Everyone should practice loyalty and bravery for the goodness of mankind.

Two Kinds:
Amy Tan

Summary: An Asian mother has different ideas and values than her daughter, which causes a struggle between the two.

Theme: Generational differences can make it difficult for families.

War of the Clowns
Mia Couto

Summary: Two clowns come to a town and start fighting each other until they get the whole town involved.

Theme: Nothing good comes from war.

Was It a Dream?
Guy de Maupassant

Summary: A man suffers immense grief after the perfect love of his life dies. He goes to visit her gravesite on a night in which all of the dead rise out of their tombs and write the truth on their tombstone. His finds his love writing that she died from catching a cold while cheating on him.

Theme: Love can cause people to believe the best about others and often masks the truth. This story would pair well with **The Chaser.**

White Lies

Erin Murphy

Summary: A young girl pretends that her father works for a candy factory in order to make friends. She has her mother buy candy every day to make up for the lie.

Theme: Bullying is wrong, just as lying and creating a false identity is wrong. This story would pair well with **Eleven.**

Zoo

Edward D. Hoch

Summary: An alien zoo travels around the universe to see unique sights.

Theme: Just because people may look different doesn't mean they are different

Comprehensive List of Poems for Grades 6 - 12
With Summaries, Themes, and Topics

A Hot Property
Ronald Wallace

Summary: The narrator discusses how he always ends up just short of being the best.

Theme: We don't always have to be the best; it is okay to be just average.

Topics: **Self-image, Beauty**

A Poison Tree
William Blake

Summary: The narrator describes how his concealed anger grew until he could get revenge upon his enemy.

Theme: Treat others as you'd want to be treated; otherwise, you might end up regretting it.

This poem would pair well with the short story, **"The Cask of Amontillado."**

Topics: **Revenge, Hatred, Poison, Ange**

A Shropshire Lad 19 To an Athlete
A.E. Housman

Summary: This poem is about a young man who wins a race and becomes the town hero. He dies soon afterward at the height of his glory.

Theme: When people die young, they will always be remembered that way.

This poem would be a good contrast to **Ex-Basketball Player.**

Topics: **Youth, Athletes, Death, Glory, Fame**

Abandoned Farmhouse
Ted Kooser

Summary: This poem describes a farmhouse which has suddenly been abandoned by the people who inhabited it.

Theme: When people aren't living up to their potential or accepting their responsibilities, sometimes it is better to move on without them.

Topics: **Nature, Responsibility, Careers, Families, Life, Abandonment**

America
Claude McKay

Summary: A man expresses his ambivalent feelings towards America in the early 1900s.

Theme: America may be the land of opportunity for some, but it hasn't always been the same for all.

Topics: **Racism, Patriotism**

Annabel Lee
Edgar Allan Poe

Summary: This poem is about the speaker's morbid obsession with a girl who died.

Theme: Love transcends anything, even death.

Topics: **Love, Obsession, Death, Youth, Nature**

Ballad of Birmingham
Dudley Randall

Summary: This poem describes the incident in Birmingham in which four girls were killed after a racial attack on a church.

Theme: No matter how much we try to protect our children, we cannot control the evil acts of others.

Topics: **Racism, Innocence, Youth, Adversity, Death**

Beware: Do Not Read This Poem
Ismael Reed

Summary: This poem is about how the things we read become a part of us.

Theme: A mirror explores how we see our true selves, so we can easily become consumed by what we think we see in the mirror.

Topics: **Vanity, Self-reflection, Beauty, Perception**

Bonny Barbara Allan
Unknown

Summary: This poem describes a man who loses his will to live because the woman he loves does not return his feelings.

Theme: It is better to let go of bitterness and forgive transgressions in order to live a happier life.

Topics: **Love, Resentment, Bitterness, Death**

Boy at the Window
Richard Wilbur

Summary: This is a poem emphasizing the ironic situation of a boy who is safe and warm worrying about a snowman outside in the elements and a snowman in his element worried about the boy.

Theme: Perception is reality.

Topics: **Innocence, Youth, Perception, Nature**

Casey at the Bat
Earnest Lawrence Thayer

Summary: This poem describes the last inning of a baseball game, which the team of Mudville is losing. The team's win or loss depends on their best player named Casey.

Theme: No one should be overconfident or arrogant about his abilities.

Topics: **Sports, Conceit, Narcissism, Defeat**

Conquerors
Henry Treece

Summary: The speaker describes his experience as he travels through a war-torn village.

Theme: Being a conqueror is not always a positive thing.

Topics: **War, Death, Devastation, Reality**

Daybreak
Jack London

Summary: This is a humorous poem which mimics Romeo and Juliet but has a surprise ending.

Theme: Things aren't always as they seem.

Topics: **Love, Misunderstandings, Life, Reality**

Deer Hit
Jon Loomis

Summary: A seventeen-year-old gives a vivid description of how he hit a deer with his car and tried to save it.

Theme: Teenagers don't always make the right decisions, and sometimes parents have to help make things right.

Topics: **Nature, Adolescence, Family, Accidents, Responsibility**

Deserted Farm
Mark Vinz

Summary: This poem gives a vivid description of an abandoned barn.

Thesis: There is beauty in everything.

This poem pairs well with the poem, **"Abandoned Farmhouse."**

Topics: **Nature, Beauty, Farms, Abandonment**

Dharma
Billy Collins

Summary: A man describes the unconditional love and adoration of his dog.

Theme: In your dog's eyes, you are a god.

This poem could pair with the poem, **"Every Cat Has a Story."**

Topics: **Animals, Friendship, Love**

Diving Into the Wreck
Adrienne Rich

Summary: A woman describes her underwater dive as she explores a shipwreck.

Theme: The quiet, serene, dark, depth of the ocean is a great equalizer between the living and the dead.

Topics: **Individualism, Isolation, Independence, Self-discovery, Nature**

Do not go gentle into that good night
Dylan Thomas

Summary: The speaker is saying that people should live life to the fullest up until the very end.

Theme: Life is short, and people should not take it for granted.

Topics: **Life, Family, Individuality, Death**

Every Cat Has a Story
Naomi Shihab Nye

Summary: The narrator describes something about each of her cats.

Theme: Cats are all unique.

This poem would pair well with the poem, **"Dharma."**

Topics: **Animals, Independence, Individuality**

Ex-Basketball Player
John Updike

Summary: This poem is about a former small-town sports hero who now works at the local gas station and remembers his glory days.

Theme: It is important to move on in life and not cling to the past.

This poem has paired questions with the poem, **"Foul Shot."**

Topics: **Sports, Careers, Loss, Heroes, Glory, Acceptance**

Facing It
Yusef Komunyakaa

Summary: A war veteran describes his feelings and observations as he visits the Vietnam Veterans Memorial.

Theme: It is impossible to escape the events from our past.

Topics: **War, Loss, Death, Family**

Fifteen
William Stafford

Summary: This poem is about a fifteen-year-old boy who finds a motorcycle and must make the adult decision of taking it and riding away or returning it to the owner who had a wreck on it.

Theme: The theme is the importance of taking responsibility and facing reality rather than being impulsive.

Topics: **Responsibility, Impulsivity, Freedom, Adolescence**

Fire and Ice
Robert Frost

Summary: The poet is saying that both fire and ice have the capacity to destroy the world.

Theme: Human beings are capable of feeling both hatred and desire and both are destructive if not controlled.

Topics: **Humans, Nature, Hatred, Destruction**

Fourteen Hundred Ninety-Two (The Re-write)
Dana W. Hall

Summary: The narrator emphasizes the historical truth about Columbus rather than the false idealism that we've been taught.

Theme: We should learn the truth about people before idealizing them.

This poem pairs well with the article, **"Goodbye, Columbus."**

Topics: **History, Heroes, Change, Conquerors**

Foul Shot
Edwin A. Hoey

Summary: A boy makes a game-winning shot at the foul line in the last sixty seconds of a game.

Theme: Live for the moment.

This poem has paired questions with the poem, **"Ex-Basketball Player."**

Topics: **Glory, Anticipation, Heroes, Sports**

Friends in the Klan 1923
Marilyn Nelson

Summary: This poem describes when a hospital was built for black veterans and how the KKK warned George Washington Carver not to attend. Carver ignored the warnings and prayed for the Klan member.

Theme: Sometimes it's impossible to change the hearts of men. It is important to fight for things we truly believe in.

Topics: **Racism, Loyalty, Protesting, History, Heroes**

Hanging Fire
Audre Lorde

Summary: A fourteen-year-old girl struggles with adolescence without the help of her mother.

Theme: Being a teenager is not easy, but adolescence eventually ends and life gets better.

Topics: **Adolescence, Adversity, Independence, Family**

Hoods
Paul B. Janeczko

Summary: The narrator describes seeing a crime take place and how he narrowly escaped being caught by the criminals.

Theme: If you think before you act, it might end up saving you.

Topics: **Crime, Criminals, Fear, Violence, Witnesses**

I Am Offering This Poem
Jimmy Santiago Baca

Summary: The speaker of the poem is expressing his love for someone by offering the only thing he has.

Theme: The best gift you can give someone is part of yourself.

Topics: **Love, Admiration, Giving**

I Ask My Mother to Sing
Li-Young Lee

Summary: A family reminisces through music of their lives in China.

Theme: Appreciate what you have at every moment, because you never know where life will take you.

Topics: **Family, Nostalgia, Comfort, Home, Memories**

I Hear America Singing
Walt Whitman

Summary: The poet describes the many different people which make up the great country of America.

Theme: America is comprised of all different types of unique individuals and that's what makes it great.

This poem pairs with **I, Too** by Langston Hughes.

Topics: **Patriotism, Individualism, Freedom**

I, Too
Langston Hughes

Summary: The poet addresses the message in Whitman's poem by pointing out that he is a black man in American and doesn't have the same privileges as other Americans.

Theme: America should mean equality for every person.

This poem pairs with Walt Whitman's **I Hear America Singing.**

Topics: **Inequality, Racism, Adversity**

I Wandered Lonely as a Cloud
William Wordsworth

Summary: The speaker reminisces about his walks through nature.

Theme: Beauty and tranquility can be found in the simplest of things.

Topics: **Nature, Peace, Life**

I Was a Skinny Tomboy Kid
Alma Luz Villanueva

Summary: The speaker describes how she was a tomboy growing up and felt like she had to protect herself from the world.

Theme: The world can be a scary place and sometimes a girl has to act tough to overcome it.

Topics: **Individuality, Independence**

Identity
Julio Noboa Polanco

Summary: The poet uses nature to describe the importance of independence.

Theme: It is better to be like an ugly weed which grows wherever it wants than a beautiful flower that is confined to one spot.

Topics: **Nature, Independence, Individualism, Freedom**

In Flanders Field
John McCrae

Summary: The speaker reflects on the lives of those who died in the war.

Theme: Nature is oblivious to the conflict of men, and life goes on without us.

Topics: **Life, Death, War, Nature, Conflict**

Junkyards
Julian Lee Rayford

Summary: The poem describes how many things are created for our convenience only to be discarded later.

Theme: Progress and technology may be destroying the earth.

Topics: **Technology, Convenience, Materialism, Progress**

Knoxville, Tennessee
Nikki Giovanni

Summary: The speaker describes the comforts of home.

Theme: There is no place like home.

Topics: **Family, Nature, Love, Comforts, Home**

Madam and the Rent Man
Langston Hughes

Summary: This poem is about a woman complaining to her landlord that she can't pay the rent but doesn't think she should have to because of the terrible conditions.

Theme: Every person has a right to be treated with dignity.

Topics: **Family, Ethics, Morality, Adversity**

Miracles
Walt Whitman

Summary: The speaker points out that miracles are everywhere is we just look around.

Theme: We should appreciate even the small things in life that we tend to overlook.

Topics: **Nature, Miracles, Appreciation, Life**

Mother to Son
Langston Hughes

Summary: A mother describes the difficulty of life with the metaphor of stairs.

Theme: Don't give up when the chips are down.

Topics: **Family, Advice, Love,**

My Papa's Waltz
Theodore Roethke

Summary: A man remembers back to when he was a boy and danced with his drunk father in the kitchen.

Theme: Our memories of the past are affected by our perceptions as children.

Topics: **Family, Dysfunctional Family, Innocence, Youth**

New Eyes
Adrienne Jaeger

Summary: A girl walking through town judges a homeless man until she sees the worn books that he has read and realizes that she shouldn't judge people.

Theme: We should never judge people based on appearances.

Topics: **Prejudice, Bias, Acceptance, Judgement**

Night Shift
Susan Kinsolving

Summary: The narrator remembers how hard she used to work in a factory and how good she felt each day when her shift was over.

Theme: Sometimes our best memories are of overcoming difficult situations.

Topics: **Work, Careers, Memories**

Nothing Gold Can Stay
Robert Frost

Summary: The poem describes how nothing stays the same and signifies that beauty fades.

Theme: Life goes on.

Topics: **Innocence, Youth, Beauty, Resilience, Time**

Ode to Family Photographs
Gary Soto

Summary: The narrator describes his mother's bad photography skills but how happy the children were in the pictures.

Theme: Life is about living in the moment.

Topics: **Family, Memories, Nostalgia, Photographs**

Poem 134: Ode to Dirt
Sharon Olds

Summary: The speaker is using the literary device of apostrophe to speak to dirt and apologize for not acknowledging and appreciating what it contributes to human life.

Theme: We shouldn't take nature and how much it contributes to life for granted.

Topics: **Nature, Life, Appreciation**

Purgatory
Maxine Kumin

Summary: The speaker gives a humorous description of what life would be like for Romeo and Juliet if they had lived.

Theme: Life doesn't always turn out like we plan.

Topics: **Family, Reality, Time, Adulthood**

Seeing the World
Steven Herrick

Summary: The narrator describes spending time with his dad and brother watching the world from the roof of their house.

Theme: The best things in life are free.

Topics: **Nature, Appreciation, Family, Nostalgia**

Shoulder
Shihab Nye

Summary: This poem describes the intense love and protection a father feels for his son.

Theme: If everyone treated each other as protective as this man for his son, the world would be a much different place.

Topics: **Family, Love, Appreciation, Innocence**

Speak Up
Janet S. Wong

Summary: An exchange between two people points out how people are sometimes unknowingly biased.

Theme: Think before you speak to make sure that you aren't offending someone.

Topics: **Bias, Prejudice, Conflict, Conversation**

Spring Storm
Jim Wayne Miller

Summary: The narrator compares an angry male to a spring storm.

Theme: Anger can be as swift and destructive as a storm.

Topics: **Anger, Personalities, Nature**

Stories
Paul B. Janeczko

Summary: An old man tells fictitious stories about his past, but when his listeners discover that he is lying they decide that they like his stories better than the truth.

Theme: Sometimes lies make good entertainment.

Topics: **Entertainment, Lies, Uniqueness, Individualism**

Street Painting
Ann Turner

Summary: The narrator describes the process a man goes through to do a street painting.

Theme: Sometimes an artist has to unlock his mind to release his art.

Topics: **Nature, Art, Individualism, Beauty**

Summertime Sharing
Nikki Grimes

Summary: The narrator describes buying an ice cream and sharing it with her friend because her friend cannot afford one.

Theme: Everything is better when shared with a friend.

Topics: **Friendship, Love, Companionship, Childhood, Sharing**

Tending
Elizabeth Alexander

Summary: A girl remembers the comforting love of her grandfather's presence when she and

her brother were young.

Theme: There are people in our lives that have an incomparable presence that cannot be forgotten.

Topics: **Family, Love, Youth, Innocence, Growth**

The Lamb and the Tyger
William Blake

Summary: The poet compares the innocence of a lamb to the fierceness of a tiger.

Theme: Everything in nature should be admired and appreciated whether it's the innocence of a lamb or the fierceness of a tiger.

Topics: **Nature, Good versus Evil, Innocence, Christianity**

The Little Boy
Helen E. Buckley

Summary: This is a poem about a little boy who loses his creativity due to the rigid constraints on a teacher.

Theme: Celebrate differences in people.

Topics: **Art, Creativity, Individualism, Conformity, Loss of innocence**

The Lorelei
Heinrich Heine

Summary: This is a lyric poem from a German legend about a girl who ends her life by jumping off a cliff because she has been jilted by her lover. Since then, the legend says that sailors have heard her singing at a bend in the river, which leads them to die among the rocks.

Theme: Life should not be taken for granted. Also, people should not trust something that seems too good to be true.

Topics: **Love, Loss, Manipulation**

The More Loving One
W.H. Auden

Summary: The speaker uses extended metaphor to compare loving someone without reciprocation.

Theme: It's not uncommon for people to love a person who doesn't feel the same, but it is important that they accept it and move on.

Topics: **Love, Unrequited Love, Nature, Acceptance**

The Past
Michael Ryan

Summary: This poem describes how unexpectedly and violently the past invades a man's day.

Theme: The past has a negative effect on many people, but they shouldn't let it control their lives.

Topics: **Trauma, Anger, Overcoming Adversity**

The Red Sweater
Joseph O. Legaspi

Summary: A young man admires his new sweater and acknowledges the hard-work it took his mother to earn the money for it.

Theme: It is necessary to acknowledge the sacrifice of your parents.

Topics: **Materialism, Money, Jobs, Careers, Sacrifice**

The Sky Over My Mother's House
Jaime Manrique

Summary: The speaker in the poem describes how he feels as he walks in the garden of his mother's house.

Theme: Small parts of the past are always with us.

This poem would pair well with **The Snowfall is So Silent.**

Topics: **Family, Adversity, Nature**

The Snowfall is So Silent
Miguel de Unamuno

Summary: The poet describes the impact that snow has when we silently watch it.

Theme: We can take comfort in nature.

This poem would pair well with **The Sky Over My Mother's House.**

Topics: **Nature, Innocence, Beauty**

the sonnet – ballad
Gwendolyn Brooks

Summary: The speaker is lamenting the fact that her lover is about to leave for war, and she knows he will never be the same.

Theme: War changes everyone. Men will do things they otherwise wouldn't in order to be a hero.

Topics: **Love, Sacrifice, Heroism, War, Adversity**

The Wreck of the Hesperus
Henry Wadsworth Longfellow

Summary: A skipper takes his daughter with him on a voyage and refuses to sail into port even though a hurricane is coming.

Theme: Those who have too much pride and arrogance are bound to suffer consequences.

Topics: **Nature, Family, Sacrifice, Pride, Death**

Theme for English B
Langston Hughes

Summary: A young African American is assigned an essay by his white professor, and he struggles with what to write.

Theme: It is important to understand our differences, but we need to realize that fundamentally we are all the same.

Topics: **Segregation, Racism, Individuality, Self-realization, Education**

To Be of Use
Marge Piercy

Summary: The speaker is describing the type of people who are useful.

Theme: A task that is done satisfactorily will not need praise or acclaim.

Topics: **Materialism, Appreciation, Individualism**

Tugboat at Daybreak
Lillian Morrison

Summary: This poem describes a tugboat first thing in the morning.

Theme: There is beauty in everything.

Topics: **Nature, Beauty, Boats**

We Wear the Mask
Paul Laurence Dunbar

Summary: The speaker discusses the "mask" people wear on their face in spite of the pain or anger that they are feeling.

Theme: People don't always show their true feelings.

Topics: **Happiness, Sadness, Regret, Life**

When Giving is All We Have
Alberto Rios

Summary: This poem is about the importance of giving.

Theme: When we give something of ourselves, we are better for it.

Topics: **Love, Sacrifice, Materialism**

Wirers
Siegfried Sassoon

Summary: A group of soldiers is assigned a dangerous mission to fix wires during World War I.

Theme: Men in war are asked to risk their lives for their country but often don't feel appreciated for their skill and sacrifice.

Topics: **Sacrifice, Patriotism, Death, Adversity, War**

Words Are Birds
Francisco X. Alarcon

Summary: The poet describes the importance of words by comparing them to a variety of things.

Theme: Words are extremely important, so we should appreciate them and choose them carefully.

Topics: **Nature, Appreciation, Beauty**

Top 15 Literary Terms for Analysis

Allusion – A direct or indirect reference in a work of literature to a well-known person, place, or event, written work, or work of art. Allusions can be **historical, literary, religious, or mythical.**

Example: His smile is like kryptonite to me. – referencing Superman cartoon

Anaphora – Repetition of the same word or words at the beginning of two or more lines, clauses, or sentences; a scheme.

Example: <u>Persons attempting</u> to find a motive in this narrative will be prosecuted; <u>persons attempting</u> to find a moral in it will be banished; <u>persons attempting</u> to find a plot in it will be shot. – Mark Twain

Antithesis – A juxtaposition of strongly contrasting ideas; true antithetical structure demands not only opposing ideas, but also that this opposition be expressed in parallel structure; a scheme.

Example: Though <u>studious</u>, he was <u>popular</u>; though <u>argumentative</u>, he was <u>modest</u>; though <u>inflexible</u>, he was <u>candid</u>; and though <u>metaphysical</u>, yet <u>orthodox.</u> – Samuel Johnson, *London Chronicle*

Asyndeton – When elements that are usually joined by conjunctions are presented in series without the conjunctions, a scheme.

Example: *Veni, Vidi, Vici.* (I came, I saw, I conquered.) – Julius Caesar

Polysyndeton – Deliberate use of more conjunctions than is normal; a scheme.

Example: ...pursues his way, <u>and</u> swims, <u>or</u> sinks, <u>or</u> wades, <u>or</u> creeps, <u>or</u> flies. – John Milton (*Paradise Lost*)

Ethos – Persuasive appeal to an audience's sense of duty or responsibility; the qualities or values that a speaker displays in order to affect an audience.

Example: Commercials advertising the military forces.

Pathos – Persuasive appeals to the emotions of an audience.

Example: Commercials which plea for assistance for abused animals.

Logos – Persuasive appeal to an audience's sense of logic or reasoning.

Metaphor – An analogy (between two seemingly dissimilar things) identifying one object with another and ascribing one or more of the qualities of the second.

Parallelism – Similarity of structure in a pair or series of related words, phrases or clauses; a scheme.

Example:...we mutually pledge to each other our Lives, our Fortunes, and our Sacred Honor. – *The Declaration of Independence*

Irony – Contrast between what is stated explicitly and what is really meant.

Verbal Irony – The actual intent is expresses in words that carry the opposite meaning.

Situational Irony – Events turn out the opposite of what was expected; what the characters and/or readers think out to happen is not what happens.

Dramatic Irony – Facts or events are unknown to a character in a play or piece of fiction but known to the reader, audience, or other characters in the work.

Sarcasm – Satire or irony that often uses bitter and caustic language to point out shortcomings or flaws; When well done, *sarcasm* can be witty and insightful; when poorly done, its simply cruel.

Example: David Sadaris's *Me Talk Pretty One Day, Family Guy, Southpark.*

Irony Explanation

There are **3** different types of irony in literature: **dramatic, verbal**, and **situational.**

Dramatic irony is when the reader knows something that a character doesn't.

Explain why this visual representation is an example of dramatic irony:

_____

_____

Verbal irony is when a speaker says one thing but means another. Many people consider it to be sarcasm.

Explain why this visual representation is an example of verbal irony:

_____

_____

Situational irony is a situation in which there is a contrast between expectation and reality.

Explain why this visual representation is an example of situational irony:

_____

_____

Syntax

Provide two examples where there is a significant change in syntax and explain the author's purpose for each.

Simile

Provide two examples of similes in the story and explain the author's purpose for using each.

Syntax

- Provide two examples where there is a significant change in syntax and explain the author's purpose for each.

Simile

- Provide two examples of similes in the story and explain the author's purpose for using each.

Parallelism

Provide one example of parallelism in the story and explain the author's purpose for using it.

Metaphor

Provide two examples of metaphors in the story and explain the author's purpose for using each.

Imagery

Provide one example of imagery in the story and explain the author's purpose for using it.

Diction

Provide three examples of significant diction in the story. Explain the connotation which the words provide and the author's purpose for using them.

Imagery

- Provide one example of imagery in the story and explain the authors purpose for using it.

Diction

- Provide three examples of significant diction in the story. Explain the connotation which the words provide and the author's purpose for using them.

64

65

Comprehending Fiction Activity

Text Used:

Character		
What things does the reader know or infer about the main character?	What changes does the character experience?	What things does the reader know or infer about any secondary characters?

Plot and Setting		
Summarize important events from the selection.	Discuss any problems that arose and the effect that it had on the characters, setting, or situation.	Describe the setting of the selection.

67

Vocabulary and Figurative Language

Literary Device	Example from the Text	Author's Purpose

Themes and Ideas

What are lessons that this selection provided? What is the theme?	What are the social issues in the selection and why are they important?	What are the symbols from the selection and what do they represent?

from *To Kill a Mockingbird*
The Incident with Mrs. Dubose

Mrs. Dubose lived alone two doors up the street from us in a house with steep front steps and a dog-trot hall. She was very old; she spent most of each day in bed and the rest of it in a wheelchair. It was rumored that she kept a CSA pistol concealed among her numerous shawls and wraps.

Jem and I hated her. If she was on the porch when we passed, we would be raked by her wrathful gaze, subjected to **ruthless interrogation** regarding our behavior, and given a **melancholy** prediction to what we would amount to when we grew up, which was always nothing. We had long ago given up the idea of walking past her house on the opposite side of the street; that only made her raise her voice and let the whole neighborhood in on it.

We could do nothing to please her. If I said as sunnily as I could, "Hey, Mrs. Dubose," I would receive for an answer, "Don't you say hey to me, you ugly girl! You say good afternoon, Mrs. Dubose!"

She was vicious. Once she heard Jem refer to our father as "Atticus" and her reaction was **apoplectic**. Besides being the sassiest, most disrespectful mutts who ever passed her way, we were told that it was quite a pity our father had not remarried after our mother's death. A lovelier lady than our mother never lived, she said, and it was heartbreaking the way Atticus Finch let her children run wild. I did not remember our mother, but Jem did – he would tell me about her sometimes – and he went livid when Mrs. Dubose shot us this message.

Countless evenings Atticus would find Jem furious at something Mrs. Dubose had said when we went by.

"Easy does it, son," Atticus would say. "She's an old lady and she's ill. You just hold your head high and be a gentleman. Whatever she says to you, it's your job not to let her make you mad."

The day after Jem's twelfth birthday his money was burning up his pockets, so we headed for town in the early afternoon.

Mrs. Dubose was stationed on her porch when we went by.

"Where are you two going at this time of day?" she shouted. "Playing hooky, I suppose. I'll just call up the principal and tell him!" She put her hands on the wheels of her chair and executed a perfect face.

"Aw, it's Saturday, Mrs. Dubose," said Jem.

"Makes no difference if it's Saturday," she said **obscurely**. "I wonder if your father knows where you are?"

"Mrs. Dubose, we've been goin' to town by ourselves since we were this high. "Jem placed his hand palm down about two feet above the sidewalk.

"Don't you lie to me!" she yelled. "Jeremy Finch, Maudie Atkinson told me you broke down her scuppernong arbor this morning. She's going to tell your father and then you'll wish you never saw the light of day! If you aren't sent to the reform school before next week, my name's not Dubose!"

Jem, who hadn't been near Miss Maudie's scuppernong arbor since last summer, and who knew Miss Maudie wouldn't tell Atticus if he had, issued a general denial.

"Don't you **contradict** me!" Mrs. Dubose bawled. "And *you* –" she pointed an arthritic finger at me – "what are you doing in those overalls? You should be in a dress and camisole, young lady! You'll grow up waiting on tables if somebody doesn't change your ways – a Finch waiting on tables at the O.K. Café – hah!"

I was terrified. The O.K. Café was a dim organization on the north side of the square. I grabbed Jem's hand, but he shook me loose.

"Come on, Scout," he whispered. "Don't pay any attention to her, just hold your head high and be a gentleman."

"Yes, indeed, what has this world come to when a Finch goes against his raising? I'll tell you!" She put her hand to her mouth. When she drew it away, it trailed a long silver thread of saliva. "Your father's no better than the trash he works for!"

I wasn't sure what Jem resented most, but I took **umbrage** at Mrs. Dubose's assessment of the family's mental hygiene. I had become almost accustomed to hearing insults aimed at Atticus. But this was the first one coming from an adult.

Jem bought his steam engine, and we went by Elmore's for my baton. On the way home, ...when we approached Mrs. Dubose's house my baton was grimy from having picked it up out of the dirt so many times.

She was not on the porch.

In later years, I sometimes wondered exactly what made Jem do it, what made him break the bonds of "You just be a gentleman, son," and the phrase of self-conscious **rectitude** he had recently entered.

What Jem did was something I'd do as a matter of course had I not been under Atticus's interdict, which I assumed included not fighting horrible old ladies. We had just come to her gate when Jem snatched my baton and ran flailing wildly up the steps into Mrs. Dubose's front yard, forgetting everything Atticus had said, forgetting that she packed a pistol under her shawls....

He did not begin to calm down until he had cut the tops off every camellia bush Mrs. Dubose owned, until the ground was littered with green buds and leaves. He bent my baton against his knee, snapped it in two and threw it down.

We did not choose to meet Atticus coming home that evening. We **skulked** around the kitchen until Calpurnia threw us out. She did give Jem a hot biscuit-and-butter which he tore in half and shared with me. It tasted like cotton.

Two geological ages later, we heard the soles of Atticus's shoes scrape the front steps. The screen door slammed, there was a pause – Atticus was at the hat rack in the hall –and we heard him call, "Jem!" His voice was like the winter wind.

Atticus switched on the ceiling light in the living room and found us there, frozen still. He carried my baton in one hand; its filthy yellow tassel trailed on the rug. He held out his other hand; it contained fat camellia buds.

"Jem," he said, "are you responsible for this?"

"Yes, sir."

"Why'd you do it?"

Jem said softly, "She said you lawed for trash."

"You did this because she said that?"

Jem's lips moved, but his "Yes sir" was inaudible.

"Son, I have no doubt that you've been annoyed by your contemporaries about me, but to do something like this to a sick old lady is inexcusable. I strongly advise you to go down and have a talk with Mrs. Dubose," said Atticus. "Come straight home afterward."

When Jem returned, he found me in Atticus's lap. "Well, son?" said Atticus. He set me on my feet, and I made a secret **reconnaissance** of Jem. He seemed to be all in one piece, but he had a queer look on his face. Perhaps she had given him a dose of calomel.

"I cleaned it up for her and said I was sorry, but I ain't, and that I'd work on 'em ever Saturday and try to make 'em grow back out."

"There was no pint in saying you were sorry if you aren't," said Atticus. "Jem, she's old and ill. You can't hold her responsible for what she does. Of course, I'd rather she'd have said it to me than to either of you, but we can't always have our druthers."

Jem seemed fascinated by a rose in the carpet. "Atticus," he said, "she wants me to read to her."

"Read to her?"

"Yes sir. She wants me to come every afternoon after school and Saturdays and read to her out loud for two hours. Atticus, do I have to?"

"Certainly."

"But she wants me to do it for a month."

"Then you'll do it for a month."

Jem planted his big toe delicately in the center of the rose and pressed it in. Finally, he said, "Atticus, it's all right on the sidewalk but inside it's – it's all dark and creepy. There's shadows and things on the ceiling...."

Atticus smiled grimly. "That should appeal to your imagination. Just pretend you're inside the Radley house."

Comprehending Fiction Answers

Text Used: Jem's Interaction with Mrs. Dubose in *To Kill a Mockingbird*

Character		
What things does the reader know or infer about the main character?	What changes does the character experience?	What things does the reader know or infer about any secondary characters?
Jem is a twelve-year-old boy who doesn't like his neighbor, Mrs. Dubose. His father is Atticus and the narrator is most likely his sister. Their mother died several years ago. Jem has been taught manners by his father and is generous based on the fact that he spent his birthday money buying something for his sister as well as himself.	Jem loses his patience and manners due to Mrs. Dubose's continual abuse of the children and the insults about his father. He destroys her camellia bushes due to his anger and readily admits it. He does not regret it because he doesn't understand why Mrs. Dubose is so mean.	Mrs. Dubose is a rude and angry character who lashes out at children. She sits on her front porch wrapped in a shawl and is rumored to carry a gun under it. The reader knows that she is very old, disabled, and ill but doesn't know the extent of it.

Plot and Setting		
Summarize important events from the selection.	Discuss any problems that arose and the effect that it had on the characters, setting, or situation.	Describe the setting of the selection.
Jem and the narrator walk to town to spend Jem's birthday money and pass the rude neighbor. She insults their father and Jem loses his temper, ruining her camellia bushes.	Mrs. Dubose's attitude is a problem to the characters, setting, and situation. The readers don't know why she is so rude and mean to the children. She causes Jem to act in a way that isn't his normal nature. The setting is changed because Jem does damage to the beautiful flowers which make up her yard. As a result, Jem has to go read to her for a month. Jem is not able to contain his intense anger due to the abuse of Mrs. Dubose, so he acts out and forgets that he is supposed to be a gentleman.	The reader can infer that they live in a small town because the children walk to town. Based on some of the terminology, "scuppernong," it appears that the setting takes place in the past. The children probably don't have much money based on the way the narrator is dressed.

Vocabulary and Figurative Language

Literary Device	Example from the Text	Author's Purpose
Diction	Words at the beginning of the selection such as, "hated, wrathful, ruthless" create a negative feeling.	The author is attempting to set up an atmosphere of negativity and discomfort that the children experience around Mrs. Dubose
Simile	"It tasted like cotton" is a simile that narrator uses to describe the biscuit that Jem gave her.	The author uses this description to emphasize the terrible feelings that the children have after their experience.
Simile	"His voice was like the winter wind" is a simile the narrator uses to describe Atticus's anger.	The author uses this description to exemplify the disappointment Atticus feels for Jem's actions.
Hyperbole	"Two geological ages later" is a hyperbole the narrator uses to describe the period the children wait for Atticus to come home.	The author uses this description to accentuate the extreme anxiety the children feel waiting for their punishment.
Idiom	"...his money was burning a hole in his pocket" is an idiom used by the narrator to describes Jem's excitement.	The author uses this description to show Jem's impatience for wanting to spend his birthday money.

Themes and Ideas

What are lessons that this selection provided? What is the theme?	What are the social issues in the selection and why are they important?	What are the symbols from the selection and what do they represent?
The lesson is that we shouldn't let other people affect the way we feel or act.	The social issue, although subtle in this part, is the fact that Atticus works for people of color and Mrs. Dubose finds that disturbing. She insults the children's father and Jem feels a need to defend his father.	Mrs. Dubose represents the racism of society during that time period (1930's.) Jem and the narrator (Scout) represent innocence and the failure to understand racism. Atticus represents honor and doing the right thing despite the circumstances. The destruction of the flowers represents the end of innocence.

1. How would you describe Mrs. Dubose from the first paragraph?

2. What diction in the second paragraph creates the negative feelings about Mrs. Dubose?

3. Based on information the narrator gives in the fourth paragraph, what can you infer about Atticus Finch's relation to the children?

4. Why does Jem tell Scout to be a gentleman while Mrs. Dubose is harassing them?

5. What did Jem buy Scout with his birthday money? What does the fact that he bought Scout something along with himself tell you about his character?

6. Why do you think Jem attacked Mrs. Dubose's bushes?

7. What literary device is Scout using when she says. "It tasted like cotton," and what does she mean by this?

8. What did Mrs. Dubose say about Atticus that made Jem so angry?

9. What consequence did Jem receive for ruining Mrs. Dubose's bushes?

10. Was Jem sorry for what he had done?

From *To Kill a Mockingbird*
The Incident with Mrs. Dubose
Vocabulary Identification Chart

Based on context clues in the excerpt, write the correct word next to each definition: **Ruthless, Interrogation, Melancholy, Apoplectic, Obscurely, Contradict, Umbrage, Rectitude, Skulked, Reconnaissance.**

Vocabulary Word	Definition
	a feeling of pensive sadness, typically with no obvious cause
	keep out of sight, typically with a sinister or cowardly motive.
	in a way that is not clear or is difficult to understand or see
	having or showing no pity or compassion for others
	offense or annoyance
	a preliminary survey to gain information; an exploratory military survey of enemy territory
	deny the truth of (a statement) by asserting the opposite
	overcome with anger; extremely indignant
	a verbal questioning of someone
	morally correct behavior or thinking; righteousness

From *To Kill a Mockingbird*
The Incident with Mrs. Dubose
Author's Craft/Purpose Questions Answers

1. How would you describe Mrs. Dubose from the first paragraph?
   She is an old woman who is not in good health. Based on the fact that she is rumored to hide a gun, she probably knows how to take care of herself.

2. What diction in the second paragraph creates the negative feelings about Mrs. Dubose?
   The negative words include "Nothing," "Melancholy," "Ruthless," "Wrathful," and "Hatred."

3. Based on information the narrator gives in the fourth paragraph, what can you infer about Atticus Finch's relation to the children?
   Atticus Finch is the children's father. Their mother died when they were young, so he has had to raise them himself.

4. Why does Jem tell Scout to be a gentleman while Mrs. Dubose is harassing them?
   Jem tells Scout to hold her head up and be a gentleman because that is what Atticus told him to do when Mrs. Dubose speaks to them.

5. What did Jem buy Scout with his birthday money? What does the fact that he bought Scout something along with himself tell you about his character?
   Jem bought Scout a baton because he felt like he should buy her something since he had money left over. This tells readers that Jem was a responsible and caring young man.

6. Why do you think Jem attacked Mrs. Dubose's bushes?
   Jem could probably take her insulting him, but Jem couldn't stand the fact that she was insulting his father.

7. What literary device is Scout using when she says. "It tasted like cotton," and what does she mean by this?
   Scout is using a simile to describe the biscuit half that Jem gave her. She can't enjoy it because she is upset about Jem's incident with Mrs. Dubose.

8. What did Mrs. Dubose say about Atticus that made Jem so angry?
   Mrs. Dubose claimed that Atticus was protecting trashy people as a lawyer.

9. What consequence did Jem receive for ruining Mrs. Dubose's bushes?
   Jem has to go read to her for a month.

10. Was Jem sorry for what he had done?
    Jem was not sorry for what he had done to Mrs. Dubose's bushes. He felt that she had no right to say the things about Atticus that she had said.

From *To Kill a Mockingbird*
The Incident with Mrs. Dubose
Vocabulary Identification Chart Answers

Based on context clues in the excerpt, write the correct word next to each definition: **Ruthless, Interrogation, Melancholy, Apoplectic, Obscurely, Contradict, Umbrage, Rectitude, Skulked, Reconnaissance.**

Vocabulary Word	Definition
Melancholy	a feeling of pensive sadness, typically with no obvious cause
Skulked	keep out of sight, typically with a sinister or cowardly motive.
Obscurely	in a way that is not clear or is difficult to understand or see
Ruthless	having or showing no pity or compassion for others
Umbrage	offense or annoyance
Reconnaissance	a preliminary survey to gain information; an exploratory military survey of enemy territory
Contradict	deny the truth of (a statement) by asserting the opposite
Apoplectic	overcome with anger; extremely indignant
Interrogation	a verbal questioning of someone
Rectitude	morally correct behavior or thinking; righteousness

To Kill a Mockingbird Excerpt

Maycomb was an old town, but it was a tired old town when I first knew it. In rainy weather, the streets turned to red slop; grass grew on the sidewalks, the courthouse sagged in the square. Somehow, it was hotter then: a black dog suffered on a summer's day; bony mules hitched to Hoover carts flicked flies in the sweltering shade of the live oaks on the square. Men's stiff collars wilted by nine in the morning. Ladies bathed before noon, after their three o'clock naps, and by nightfall were life soft teacakes with frosting of sweat and sweet talcum.

People moved slowly then. They ambled across the square, shuttled in and out of the stored around it, took their time about everything. A day was twenty-four hours long but seemed longer. There was no hurry for there was nowhere to go, nothing to buy, and no money to buy it with, nothing to see outside of the boundaries of Maycomb. But it was a time of vague optimism for some of the people. Maycomb County had recently been told that it had nothing to fear but fear itself.

What message (author's purpose) was the author trying to convey with this passage?

What techniques (author's craft) does the author use to convey his message?

To Kill a Mockingbird Maycomb Passage Analysis Questions

1. What does the narrator mean when she calls Maycomb a "tired old town" and what does she mean by "...when I first knew it"?

2. What does she mean when she says, "...grass grew on the sidewalks and the courthouse sagged in the square"?

3. Which literary term is she using when she says, "...a black dog suffered on a summer's day; bony mules hitched to Hoover carts flicked flies in the sweltering shade of the live oaks on the square"?

4. Which literary term is the narrator using when she says, "Ladies...were like soft teacakes with frosting and sweat and sweet talcum"?

5. What does the author mean when she says, "People moved slowly then"?

6. "They ambled across the square, shuttled in and out of stores around it, took their time about everything." What does the word "ambled" mean and why is it so effective in this sentence?

7. What literary device is the author using when she says, "...there was nowhere to go, nothing to buy, and no money to buy it with..."?

8. *To Kill a Mockingbird* took place from 1933 – 1935. What does the sentence from question seven tell the reader about the time period in America? What is that time period referring to?

9. What literary device is the narrator using when she says, "...had recently been told that it had nothing to fear but fear itself"?

10. How are these two paragraphs important for establishing a setting for the story?

To Kill a Mockingbird Maycomb Passage Analysis Answers

1. What does the narrator mean when she calls Maycomb a "tired old town" and what does she mean by "...when I first knew it"?

    By using the word "tired" to describe Maycomb, the author is saying that the town never changes. By saying, "... when I first knew it, the narrator is insinuating that she was a child at the time and it probably still hasn't changed.

2. What does she mean when she says, "...grass grew on the sidewalks and the courthouse sagged in the square"?

    The author uses imagery to describe the town and indicates that the people don't take pride in their community because it is allowed to decay.

3. Which literary term is she using when she says, "...a black dog suffered on a summer's day; bony mules hitched to Hoover carts flicked flies in the sweltering shade of the live oaks on the square"?

    The author uses alliteration imagery to provide a vivid and accurate portrayal of Maycomb at the time the story is taking place.

4. Which literary term is the narrator using when she says, "Ladies...were like soft teacakes with frosting and sweat and sweet talcum"?

    The author is using a sense of sight, smell, and touch with imagery to pull the reader into the story.

5. What does the author mean when she says, "People moved slowly then"?

    People were more laid back and didn't have as many concerns. They didn't have money, so they just lived life day to day getting by the best they could.

6. "They ambled across the square, shuttled in and out of stores around it, took their time about everything." What does the word "ambled" mean and why is it so effective in this sentence?

    Ambled means walking or moving at a slow pace. It is a great word to describe the movement of the people at that time because no one was in a hurry.

7. What literary device is the author using when she says, "...there was nowhere to go, nothing to buy, and no money to buy it with..." and what is the purpose of it?

    The author is using parallelism to exemplify the mundane and somewhat joyless existence the people had at the time.

8. *To Kill a Mockingbird* took place from 1933 – 1935. What does the sentence from question seven tell the reader about the time period in America? What is that time period referring to?

That time period is referred to as The Great Depression because America experienced an extreme recession after The Stock Market Crash. Jobs and food were scarce, so most Americans were having a very rough time.

9. What literary device is the narrator using when she says, "...had recently been told that it had nothing to fear but fear itself"?

This statement is a historical allusion referring to Franklin Delano Roosevelt's 1933 inaugural speech when he tried to comfort the nation.

10. How are these two paragraphs important for establishing a setting for the story?

These paragraphs exemplify what was going on in the country at the time. People were worried about their own survival and less apt to be concerned about their fellow man. This probably added to the racism at the time and the fact that the innocent Tom Robinson in the story was wrongly convicted of a horrible crime.

How to Analyze a Text for Author's Purpose

This is a step-by-step process to help teachers analyze and create higher-level thinking questions for author's purpose.

Step One
If the text is non-fiction, especially a speech, find out as much background information as possible so that you know the purpose of it.

Read through the passage as many times as it takes until you have a central idea of what the passage is saying.

Read through the passage and circle any words you think the students might not understand.

Step Two
Choose a highlighter and highlight and label all of the literary devices that the author used.

Step Three
Choose a different highlighter and highlight anything that stands out as unusual, questionable, or interesting. Write down any notes about those things, whether it's a question or comment. (This will get easier the more you practice it.)

Step Four
Based on your annotations from the text, create questions to lead a discussion with students.

Step One

To Kill a Mockingbird Excerpt

Maycomb was an old town, but it was a tired old town when I first knew it. In rainy weather the streets turned to red slop; grass grew on the sidewalks, the courthouse sagged in the square. Somehow, it was hotter then: a black dog suffered on a summer's day; bony mules hitched to Hoover carts flicked flies in the sweltering shade of the live oaks on the square. Men's stiff collars wilted by nine in the morning. Ladies bathed before noon, after their three o'clock naps, and by nightfall were life soft teacakes with frostings of sweat and sweet talcum.

People moved slowly then. They ambled across the square, shuttled in and out of the stores around it, took their time about everything. A day was twenty-four hours long but seemed longer. There was no hurry for there was nowhere to go, nothing to buy, and no money to buy it with, nothing to see outside of the boundaries of Maycomb. But it was a time of vague optimism for some of the people. Maycomb County had recently been told that it had nothing to fear but fear itself.

What message (author's purpose) was the author trying to convey with this passage?

What techniques (author's craft) does the author use to convey his message?

To Kill a Mockingbird Excerpt

Maycomb was an old town, but it was a tired old town when I first knew it. In rainy weather the streets turned to red slop; grass grew on the sidewalks, the courthouse sagged in the square. Somehow, it was hotter then: a black dog suffered on a summer's day; bony mules hitched to Hoover carts flicked flies in the sweltering shade of the live *alliteration* oaks on the square. Men's stiff collars wilted by nine in the morning. *imagery* Ladies bathed before noon, after their three o'clock naps, and by nightfall were life soft teacakes with frostings of sweat and sweet *imagery, simile* talcum.

diction   *diction*

People moved slowly then. They ambled across the square, shuttled in and out of the stores around it, took their time about everything. A day was twenty-four hours long but seemed longer. There was no
repetition
hurry for there was nowhere to go, nothing to buy, and no money to
repetition
buy it with, nothing to see outside of the boundaries of Maycomb. But it was a time of vague optimism for some of the people. Maycomb County had recently been told that it had nothing to fear but fear itself.

What message (author's purpose) was the author trying to convey with this passage?

What techniques (author's craft) does the author use to convey his message?

Step One
Step Two
Step Three *To Kill a Mockingbird* Excerpt

never changes   *she is older now*

Maycomb was an old town, but it was a tired old town when I first
knew it. In rainy weather the streets turned to red <u>slop</u>; grass grew on   *why is it decaying?*
the sidewalks, the courthouse sagged in the square. Somehow, it was
hotter then: a black dog suffered on a summer's day; bony mules
hitched to (Hoover carts) flicked flies in the sweltering shade of the live   *alliteration*
oaks on the square. Men's stiff collars wilted by nine in the morning.   *imagery*
Ladies bathed before noon, after their three o'clock naps, and by
nightfall were life soft teacakes with frostings of sweat and sweet   *imagery, simile*
(talcum.)

literal or figurative? (left margin)

What was the difference?   *diction*   *diction*

People moved slowly then. They (ambled) across the square, shuttled
in and out of the stores around it, took their time about everything. A
day was twenty-four hours long but seemed longer. There was no
hurry for there was nowhere to go, nothing to buy, and no money to   *people were poor*
buy it with, nothing to see outside of the boundaries of Maycomb. But
it was a time of (vague) optimism for some of the people. Maycomb
County had recently been told that it had nothing to fear but fear itself.

repetition *repetition*

historical allusion FDR 1933 Inaugural Address

What message (author's purpose) was the author trying to convey
with this passage?

> *The author uses the setting to establish the message that people are resistant to change.*

What techniques (author's craft) does the author use to convey his
message?

> *The author uses imagery to help the reader comprehend the feeling of a small town where nothing happens. She develops a negative mood with the connotation of her diction with words such as "slop", "suffered", and "wilted".*

"The Gettysburg Address" By Abraham Lincoln

Background Information

The Battle of Gettysburg took place in Gettysburg, Pennsylvania during the Civil War July 1-3, 1863. 170,000 Union and Confederate soldiers fought a bloody battle. As a result, a quarter of the Union soldiers died (23,000) and a third of the Confederate soldiers died (28,000). It was a crushing defeat for the Confederacy. On November 19, 1863, a crowd of 15,000 gathered in Gettysburg to dedicate a cemetery to the soldiers killed there. The first speaker, the highly respected orator and politician Edward Everett, spoke for two hours. Lincoln followed with this famous two-minute speech. Everett later complimented Lincoln for saying in two minutes what he failed to say in two hours.

Four score and seven years ago our fathers brought forth, on this continent, a new nation, conceived in Liberty, and dedicated to the proposition that all men are created equal.

Now we are engaged in a great civil war, testing whether this nation, or any nation so conceived and so dedicated, can long endure. We are met on a great battlefield of that war. We have come to dedicate a portion of that field, as a final resting place for those who gave their lives, that that nation might live. It is altogether fitting and proper that we should do this.

But in a larger sense, we cannot dedicate – we cannot consecrate – we cannot hallow – this ground. The brave men, living and dead, who struggled here, have consecrated it, far above our poor power to add or detract. The world will little note, nor long remember what we say here, but it can never forget what they did here. It is for us living, rather, to be dedicated here to the unfinished work which they who fought here have thus far so nobly advanced. It is rather for us to be here dedicated to the great task remaining before us – that from these honored dead we take increased devotion to that cause for which they here gave the last full measure of devotion – that we here highly resolve that these dead shall not have died in vain – that this nation, under God, shall have a new birth of freedom – and that government of the people, by the people, for the people, shall not perish from the earth.

"The Gettysburg Address"
Author's Craft/Purpose Questions

1. How many years is a score? Why do you think Lincoln started the speech by saying "Four score and seven years ago..." rather than using the actual numbers?

2. At the beginning of the speech, why did Lincoln use the historical allusion, "...all men are created equal"?

3. What was the effect of Lincoln using the anaphora (repetition at the beginning of sentences) "we" in the second paragraph?

4. Why does Lincoln use the euphemism "those who gave their lives" instead of just saying "died"?

5. In the third paragraph, Lincoln begins with parallel structure and anaphora (purposefully leaving out conjunctions) for what reason?

6. What is ironic about Lincoln's statement, "The world will little note, nor long remember what we say here, but it can never forget what they did here"?

7. What is Lincoln's tone in the speech? Explain. What diction did he use to create this tone?

8. What is Lincoln's purpose for this speech? Do you think he accomplished what he set out to do? Explain.

The Gettysburg Address"
Author's Craft/Purpose Questions Answers

1. How many years is a score? Why do you think Lincoln started the speech by saying "Four score and seven years ago..." rather than using the actual numbers?
A score is 20 years. He used the phrase "Four score..." to start the speech in a formal tone rather than a casual tone. He wanted the people to know that he was serious about this occasion.

2. At the beginning of the speech, why did Lincoln use the historical allusion, "...all men are created equal"?
He was trying to establish a purpose for the many deaths to ease the suffering of the friends and relatives.

3. What was the effect of Lincoln using the anaphora (repetition at the beginning of sentences) "we" in the second paragraph?
Lincoln wants to reassure the people that he truly cares, feels that he is in this war with them and is one of them. The word "we" creates a sense of unity.

4. Why does Lincoln use the euphemism "those who gave their lives" instead of just saying "died"?
Lincoln uses a euphemism to make the deaths a little less painful and easier to accept.

5. In the third paragraph, Lincoln begins with parallel structure and anaphora (purposefully leaving out conjunctions) for what reason?
The asyndeton, or connecting the three phases without a conjunction, emphasizes the seriousness of the situation. The parallelism shows the importance of the deaths and indicates a continued admiration of the men who gave their lives.

6. What is ironic about Lincoln's statement, "The world will little note, nor long remember what we say here, but it can never forget what they did here"?
It is ironic that Lincoln felt that his speech was forgettable when we are reading and analyzing it over a hundred and fifty years later.

7. What is Lincoln's tone in the speech? Explain. What diction did he use to create this tone?
Lincoln's tone is hopeful and reverent. He is trying to give the people a reason for the deaths and a will to continue the fight while showing respect to those who died. Lincoln used words like, "dedicated," "devotion," "task," "freedom," and "God" to achieve this tone.

8. What is Lincoln's purpose for this speech? Do you think he accomplished what he set out to do? Explain.
Lincoln's purpose was to try to alleviate the pain and devastation caused by the bloody battle. He wanted to help the people but make sure they still had the will to continue fighting the war. His speech was obviously successful because it is still remembered and studied over 150 years later.

Step One
Step Two
Step Three

The Gettysburg Address
A Speech by Abraham Lincoln
November 19, 1863

Formal Why not 87 yrs?

parallelism

Four score and seven years ago our fathers brought forth on this continent, a new

metaphor · *historical allusion*

nation, conceived in Liberty, and dedicated to the proposition that all men are

created equal.

Repetition of we shows unity

anaphora · *parallelism* · *repetition*

Now we are engaged in a great civil war, testing whether that nation, or any

nation so conceived and so dedicated, can long endure. We are met on a great

battlefield of that war. We have come to dedicate a portion of that field, as a

euphemism

final resting place for those who here gave their lives that that nation might live.

It is altogether fitting and proper that we should do this. *pathos*

anaphora, parallelism, asyndeton

But in a larger sense, we cannot dedicate – we cannot consecrate – we cannot

antithesis

hallow – this ground. The brave men, living and dead, who struggled here, have

antithesis

consecrated it, far above our poor power to add or detract. The world will little *antithesis*

This statement is ironic because we are still studying it.

note, nor long remember what we say here, but it can never forget what they did

euphemism

here. It is for us the living, rather, to be dedicated here to the unfinished work

which they who fought here have thus far so nobly advanced. It is rather for us to

euphemism

be here dedicated to the great task remaining before us – that from these

honored dead we take increased devotion to that cause for which they here gave

euphemism

the last full measure of devotion – that we here highly resolve that these dead

personification

shall not have died in vain – that this nation, under God, shall have a new birth of

metaphor

parallelism · *asyndeton*

freedom – and that government of the people, by the people, for the people, shall

not perish from the earth.

euphemism

The euphemisms make the war easier to accept and not
    so painful.
The parallelism creates a pattern of normalcy, familiarity,
    and consistency to ease anxiety.
The repetition of "we" shows that he's with them.

"The Gettysburg Address"
Literary Device Identification Chart

Quote from Speech	Literary Device	Author's Purpose
"The brave men, living and dead, who struggled here, have consecrated it, far above our poor power to add or detract.		
"…and that government of the people, by the people, for the people shall not perish…"		
"increased devotion to that cause for which they here gave the last full measure of devotion…"		
"…that this nation, under God, shall have a new birth of freedom…"		
"…that this nation, under God, shall have a new birth of freedom…"		

"The Gettysburg Address"
Literary Device Identification Chart
Answers

Quote from Speech	Literary Device	Author's Purpose
"The brave men, living and dead, who struggled here, have consecrated it, far above our poor power to add or detract."	Antithesis	The use of antithesis enforces the feeling that this war was all inclusive. Everyone was affected in one way or another.
"...and that government of the people, by the people, for the people shall not perish..."	Parallelism	Lincoln wants to reinforce that the support and unity is ongoing.
"increased devotion to that cause for which they here gave the last full measure of devotion..."	Euphemism	Lincoln uses words that are less harsh to help people deal with reality while easing their pain.
"...that this nation, under God, shall have a new birth of freedom..."	Personification	Lincoln personifies the nation and gives it human-like qualities to provide unity and inspire everyone who is a part of the nation.
"...that this nation, under God, shall have a new birth of freedom..."	Metaphor	Lincoln uses a metaphor for freedom to make it seem more attainable in that it is ordained by God.

93

Examine for Author's Purpose Chart

E X	Examine the structure (syntax) and title	
A	Affirm the meaning by reading for clarity	
M	Mention the tone (author's attitude) and mood (readers feelings)	
I	Identify the author's purpose (message)	
N	Narrow down the author's word choices (diction, denotation, connotation)	
E	Evaluate the author's craft (simile, metaphor, parallelism, shifts, etc.)	

From *All Summer in a Day*
By Ray Bradbury

Margot stood apart from them, from these children who could never remember a time when there wasn't rain and rain and rain. They were all nine years old, and if there had been a day, seven years ago, when the sun came out for an hour and showed its face to the stunned world, they could not recall. Sometimes at night, she heard them stir, in remembrance, and she knew they were dreaming and remembering gold or a yellow crayon or a coin large enough to buy the world with. She knew they thought they remembered a warmness, like a blushing in the face, in the body, in the arms and legs and trembling hands. But then they always awoke to the tatting drum, the endless shaking down of clear bead necklaces upon the roof, the walk, the gardens, the forests, and their dreams were gone.

Questions:

What is the main idea of this passage?

This is a summary of the passage:

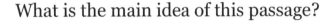

From *Dark They Were and Golden-Eyed*
By Ray Bradbury

The sun was hot, the day quiet. There was only an immense staring burn upon the land. They moved along the canal, the father, the mother, the racing children in their swimsuits. They stopped and ate meat sandwiches. He saw their skin baking brown. And he saw the yellow eyes of his wife and his children, their eyes were never yellow before. A few tremblings shook him but were carried off in waves of pleasant heat as he lay in the sun. He was too tired to be afraid.

Questions:

What is the main idea of this passage?

The following is a summary of the passage:

Which word best describes the mood of the passage?

From *A Sound of Thunder*
By Ray Bradbury

It came on great oiled, resilient, striding legs. It towered thirty feet above half of the trees, a great evil god, folding its delicate watchmaker's claws close to its oily reptilian chest. Each lower leg was a piston, a thousand pounds of white bone, sunk in thick ropes of muscle, sheathed over in a gleam of pebbled skin like the mail of a terrible warrior. Each thigh was a ton of meat, ivory, and steel mesh. And from the great breathing cage of the upper body of those two delicate arms dangled out front, arms with hands which might pick up and examine men like toys, while the snake neck coiled. And the head itself, a ton of sculptured stone, lifted easily upon the sky. Its mouth gaped, exposing a fence of teeth like daggers. Its eyes rolled, ostrich eggs, empty of all expression save hunger. It closed its mouth in a death grin. It ran, its pelvic bones crushing aside trees and bushes, its taloned feet clawing damp earth, leaving prints six inches deep wherever it settled its weight.

Questions:

Which word best describes the mood of this passage?

Which sentence gives the best clue as to what this passage is referring?

The purpose of this passage is to?

The Tyrant Lizard raised itself. Its armored flesh glittered like a thousand green coins. The coins, crusted with slime, steamed. In the slime, tiny insects wriggled, so that the entire body seemed to twitch and undulate, even while the monster itself did not move. It exhaled. The stink of raw flesh blew down the wilderness.

"Get me out of here," said Eckels. "It was never like this before. I was always sure I'd come through alive. I had good guides, good safaris, and safety. This time, I figured wrong. I've met my match and admit it. This is too much for me to get hold of."

Questions:

Which word best describes how Eckels is feeling?

What is the main idea of this passage?

This excerpt is mainly about

Details in the passage characterize the dinosaur as

Details in the passage characterize Eckels as

From *Blues Ain't No Mockin Bird*
By Toni Cade Bambara

He looks down into his chest of metal reels and things like he's protectin a kitten from the cold.

You standin in the missus' flower bed," say Granddaddy. "This is our own place."

The two men look at him, then at each other, then back at the mess in the camera man's chest, and they just back off. One sayin over and over all the way down to the meadow. "Watch it, Bruno. Keep ya fingers off the film." Then Granddaddy picks up the hammer and jams it into the oilskin pocket, scrapes his boots, and goes into the house. And you can hear the squish of his boots headin through the house. And you can see the funny shadow he throws from the parlor window into the ground by the string-bean patch. The hammer draggin the pocket of the oilskin out so Granddaddy looked even wider. Granny was hummin now – high, not low and grumbly. And she was doin the cakes again, you could smell the molasses from the rum.

Questions:

What is the main idea of this passage?

Details in the passage characterize Granddaddy as

Which word best describes the feeling of the men

From "Bread"
By Margaret Atwood

Imagine a famine. Now imagine a piece of bread. Both of these things are real but you happen to be in the same room with only one of them. Put yourself into a different room, that's what the mind is for. You are now lying on a thin mattress in a hot room. The walls are made of dried earth, and your sister, who is younger than you, is in the room with you. She is starving, her belly is bloated, flies land on her eyes; you brush them off with your hand. You have a cloth too, filthy but damp, and you press it to her lips and forehead. The piece of bread is the bread you've been saving, for days it seems. You are hungry as she is, but not yet as weak. How long does it take? When will someone come with more bread? You think of going out to see if you might find something that could be eaten, but outside the streets are infested with scavengers and the stink of corpses is everywhere.

Should you share the bread or give the whole piece to your sister? Should you eat the bread yourself? After all, you have a better chance of living, you're stronger. How long does it take to decide?

Questions:

What is the main idea of this passage?

Which word best describes the mood of the passage?

Details in the passage characterize the narrator as

From *Catch the Moon*
By Judith Ortiz Cofer

Luis Cintron sits on top of a six-foot pile of hubcaps and watches his father walk away into the steel jungle of his car junkyard. Released into his old man's custody after six months in juvenile hall – for breaking and entering – and he didn't even take anything. He did it on a dare. But the old lady with the million cats was a light sleeper, and good with her aluminum cane. He has a scar on his head to prove it.

Now Luis is wondering whether he should have stayed in and done his full time. Jorge Cintron of Jorge Cintron & Son, Auto Parts and Salvage, has decided that Luis should wash and polish every hubcap in the yard. The hill he is sitting on is only the latest couple of hundred wheel covers that have come in. Luis grunts and stands up on top of his silver mountain. He yells at no one, "Someday, son, all this will be yours," and sweeps his arms like the Pope blessing a crowd over the piles of car sandwiches and mounds of metal parts that cover this acre of land outside the city. He is the "Son" of Jorge Cintron & Son, and so far his father has had more than one reason to wish it was plain Jorge Cintron on the sign.

Luis has been getting in trouble since he started high school two years ago, mainly because of the "social group" he organized – a bunch of guys who were into harassing the local authorities. Their thing was taking something to the limit on a dare or, better still, doing something dangerous, like breaking into a house, not to steal, just to prove that they could do it. This was Luis's specialty, coming up with very complicated plans, like military strategies and assigning the "jobs" to guys who wanted to join the Tiburones.

Questions:

What is the main idea of this passage?

Which word best describes Luis's feelings about his father's business?

Details in the passage characterize Luis as

From *Catch the Moon* (2)
By Judith Ortiz Cofer

All this was going through Luis's head as he slid down the hill of hubcaps. The tub full of soapy water, the can of polish, and the bad of rags had been neatly placed in front of a makeshift table made from two car seats and a piece of plywood. Luis heard a car drive up and someone honk their horn. His father emerged from inside a new red Mustang that had been totaled. He usually dismantled every small feature by hand before sending the vehicle into the Cementerio, as he called the lot. Luis watched as the most beautiful girl he had ever seen climbed out of a vintage white Volkswagon bug. She stood in the sunlight in her white sundress waiting for his father, while Luis stared. She was like a smooth wood carving. Her skin was mahogany, almost black, and her arms and legs were long and thin, but curved in places so that she did not look bony and hard – more like a ballerina. And her ebony hair was braided close to her head. Luis let his breath out, feeling a little dizzy. He had forgotten to breathe. Both the girl and his father heard him. Mr. Cintron waved him over.

Questions:

What is the main idea of this passage?

Which phrase best exemplifies Luis's feelings toward the girl?

Details in the passage characterize Luis as

© 2024 Rohach

From *Catch the Moon* (3)
By Judith Ortiz Cofer

His father didn't answer, just handed him a set of keys, as shiny as the day they were manufactured. His father polished everything that could be polished: doorknobs, coins, keys, spoons, knives, and forks, like he was King Midas counting his silver and gold. Luis thought his father must be really lonely to polish utensils only he used anymore. They had been picked out by his wife, though they were like relics. Nothing she ever owned could be thrown away. Only now the dishes, forks, and spoons were not used to eat the yellow rice and red beans, the fried chicken, or the mouth-watering sweet plantains that his mother had cooked for them. They were just kept in the cabinets that his father turned into a museum for her. Mr. Cintron could cook as well as his wife, but he didn't have the heart to do it anymore. Luis thought that maybe if they ate together once in a while things might get better between them, but he always had something to do around dinnertime and ended up at a hamburger joint. Tonight was the first time in months they had sat down at the table together.

Questions:

What is the main idea of this passage?

Which sentence best exemplifies the way Luis's father feels about his wife?

Details in the passage characterize Mr. Cintron as

From *Death by Scrabble*
By Charlie Fish

I watch my wife's smug expression as she rearranges her letters. Clack, clack, clack. I hate her. If she wasn't around, I'd be doing something interesting right now. I'd be climbing Mount Kilimanjaro. I'd be starring in the latest Hollywood blockbuster. I'd be sailing the Vendee Globe on a 60-foot clipper called the New Horizons – I don't know, but I'd be doing something.

Questions:

Which word best describes the narrator's feelings?

The short syntax (sentence structure) is used by the author to

Dora took the gold bars to her petunia bed beside the house and buried them in the loose black soil. She paid no heed to the sound of a car coming down the highway at high speed until it passed the house and a wild squawking sounded above the roar of the motor. She hurried around to the front of the house, knowing already what had happened. She stared in dismay at the four chickens which lay dead in the road. She knew that Calvin would blame her and beat her into unconsciousness.

Fear sharpened her wits. Perhaps if she could dispose of the bodies Calvin would think foxes had got them. Hastily she gathered up the dead chickens and feathers which lay scattered about. When she was finished, there was no evidence of the disaster. She carried the chickens to the back of the house wondering how she could dispose of them. Suddenly, as she glanced towards the hole, the answer came to her.

Questions:

What is the mood of the passage?

Which words (diction) create the mood?

Which word best describes Dora's feelings?

The following is a summary of the passage:

"Annabel Lee" by Edgar Allan Poe
Author's Craft/Purpose Activity

Poem	Summary

It was many and many a year ago,
   In a kingdom by the sea,
That a maiden there lived whom you may know
   By the name of Annabel Lee; --
And this maiden she lived with no other thought
   Than to love and be loved by me.	

I was a child and *she* was a child,
   In this kingdom by the sea;
But we loved with a love that was more than love—
   I and my Annabel Lee –
With a love that the winged seraphs in Heaven
   Coveted her and me.	

And this was the reason that, long ago,
   In this kingdom by the sea,
A wind blew out of a cloud, chilling
   My beautiful Annabel Lee;
So that her high-born kinsmen came
   And bore her away from me,
To shut her up in a sepulchre,
   In this kingdom by the sea.	

The angels, not half so happy in Heaven,
   Went envying her and me –
Yes! – that was the reason (as all men know,
   In this kingdom by the sea)
That the wind came out of the cloud by night,
   Chilling and killing my Annabel Lee.	

But our love it was stronger by far than the love
   Of those who were older than we –
   Of many far wiser than we –
And neither the angels in Heaven above,
   Nor the demons down under the sea,
Can ever dissever my soul from the soul
   Of the beautiful Annabel Lee: --	

For the moon never beams, without bringing me dreams
   Of the beautiful Annabel Lee –
And the stars never rise, but I feel the bright eyes
   Of the beautiful Annabel Lee –
And so, all the night-tide, I lie down by the side
Of my darling –my darling—my life and my bride,
   In her sepulchre there by the sea –
   In her tomb by the sounding sea.	

"Annabel Lee" by Edgar Allan Poe
Author's Craft/Purpose Activity

Before Reading

1. Based on the title, what specifically do you think the poem is about?

2. Look at the poem. How many stanzas does the poem consist of? Without reading the poem, how many times do you see the name Annabel Lee within the poem?

3. What are your predictions based on what you see?

During Reading

1. Read the poem and write a summary beside each stanza.

2. For each stanza, put letters next to each line to identify the rhyme scheme. Start with A. With each new sound at the end of the line, put a new letter. For example, the first stanza should be A B A B C B.

3. What do you notice about the rhyme scheme in the poem? Are all the stanzas identical? Are any of the stanzas identical? What might this tell the reader about the speaker?

4. The last stanza is unique in that it rhymes within each line. What is the effect of this while reading the poem and why might the author have done this?

5. In the second stanza, what are the winged seraphs to which he is referring and what does he mean saying that he and Annabel Lee were coveted?

6. What does the speaker blame for the death of Annabel Lee?

7. According to stanzas three and six, what is a sepulcher?

8. How would you describe the speaker in the poem? Explain with evidence from the poem.

9. What does the speaker mean when he says in stanza five that his soul can never be "dissevered" from the soul of Annabel Lee? What type of connotation does the word "dissevered" have?

10. What is unusual about the way the speaker stays close to Annabel Lee? What does this action tell the reader about him?

After Reading

1. Was your prediction about the poem correct?

2. What do you think the author's purpose/message was with this poem?

3. Does the structure of the poem add or detract from the message of the poem? Explain.

4. Do you consider this to be a love poem? Why or why not?

"Annabel Lee" by Edgar Allan Poe
Author's Craft/Purpose Activity
Answers

Before Reading

1. Based on the title, what specifically do you think the poem is about?

   Answers will vary.

2. Look at the poem. How many stanzas does the poem consist of? Without reading the poem, how many times do you see the name Annabel Lee within the poem?

   The poem consists of six stanzas and Annabel Lee is mentioned seven times.

3. What are your predictions based on what you see?

   Answers will vary. Seeing the name Annabel Lee so many times might indicate an obsession.

During Reading

1. Read the poem and write a summary beside each stanza.

   See Teacher Copy

2. For each stanza, put letters next to each line to identify the rhyme scheme. Start with A. With each new sound at the end of the line, put a new letter. For example, the first stanza should be A B A B C B.

   See Teacher Copy

3. What do you notice about the rhyme scheme in the poem? Are all of the stanzas identical? Are any of the stanzas identical? What might this tell the reader about the speaker?

   The rhyme scheme is different in every stanza. It is similar in the first and fifth stanzas, but the fifth one has extra lines. It might indicate that the speaker is erratic or unbalanced, possibly being mentally unstable.

4. The last stanza is unique in that it rhymes within each line. What is the effect of this while reading the poem and why might the author have done this?

   The rhyme within the lines of the poem cause it to speed up. This gives the impression that the narrator is talking faster and adds to his instability.

© 2024 Rohach

5. In the second stanza, what are the winged seraphs to which he is referring and what does he mean saying that he and Annabel Lee were coveted?

   He is saying that the angels in Heaven were jealous of the love that he and Annabel Lee had.

6. What does the speaker blame for the death of Annabel Lee?

   He claims that the angels, due to envy, sent a wind that cause her to get sick and die.

7. According to stanzas three and six, what is a sepulchre?

   It is a tomb built in rock or made of stone in which people are buried.

8. How would you describe the speaker in the poem? Explain with evidence from the poem.

   The speaker is a young man who is in love with a girl who has died. He calls her a maiden which indicates that she's young, and he talks about "those who were older than we...."

9. What does the speaker mean when he says in stanza five that his soul can never be "dissevered" from the soul of Annabel Lee? What type of connotation does the word "dissevered" have?

   It is another word for separated. It has a negative connotation because it reminds readers of the word severed.

10. What is unusual about the way the speaker stays close to Annabel Lee? What does this action tell the reader about him?

    He goes to the tomb and lies beside her every night? He is probably crazy.

After Reading

1. Was your prediction about the poem correct?

   Answers will vary.

2. What do you think the author's purpose/message was with this poem?

   The author's purpose was to show that love transcends everything, even death.

3. Does the structure of the poem add or detract from the message of the poem? Explain.

   Answers will vary. It adds to the poem because the repetitiveness of certain sounds exemplifies his obsession with the young woman.

4. Do you consider this to be a love poem? Why or why not?

   Answers will vary.

"Annabel Lee" by Edgar Allan Poe
Author's Craft/Purpose Activity

	Poem	Summary

A B A B C B	It was many and many a year ago, *repetition*
	  In a kingdom by the sea,
	That a maiden there lived whom you may know
	  By the name of Annabel Lee; --
	And this maiden she lived with no other thought
	  Than to love and be loved by me. *antithesis*
	    why italics?
		The speaker is describing a girl who he loves and who loves him. Her name is Annabel Lee and she lives in a kingdom by the sea.

A B C B D B	I was a child and she was a child, *parallelism, repetition*
	  In this kingdom by the sea;
	But we loved with a love that was more than love—
	  I and my Annabel Lee – *repetition*
	With a love that the winged seraphs in Heaven
	  Coveted her and me.
		The speaker describes the love they shared as unique and one that was so intense the Angels in Heaven were jealous.

A B C B D B E B	And this was the reason that, long ago, *they had a unique love*
	  In this kingdom by the sea,
	A wind blew out of a cloud, chilling
	  My beautiful Annabel Lee;
	So that her high-born kinsmen came
	  And bore her away from me,
	To shut her up in a sepulchre, *Did she die?*
	  In this kingdom by the sea.
		The speaker believes that due to the angels' jealousy, a cold wind caused Annabel to get sick and die. Her relatives buried her in a tomb next to the sea.

A B C B D B	The angels, not half so happy in Heaven,
	  Went envying her and me – *Why are they jealous?*
	Yes! – that was the reason (as all men know,
	  In this kingdom by the sea)
	That the wind came out of the cloud by night,
	  Chilling and killing my Annabel Lee. *personification*
		The speaker reiterates that the angels' jealousy of their love and happiness is what caused the cold wind to blow and kill her.

A B B A B C B	But our love it was stronger by far than the love *repetition*
	  Of those who were older than we –
	  Of many far wiser than we –
	And neither the angels in Heaven above,
	  Nor the demons down under the sea,
	Can ever dissever my soul from the soul *repetition*
	  Of the beautiful Annabel Lee: --
		The speaker claims that the love they shared was stronger than even those who are older and wiser. Nothing can stop the unique care and devotion they have for each other.

A B C B D D B B	For the moon never beams, without bringing me dreams *parallelism*
	  Of the beautiful Annabel Lee –
	And the stars never rise, but I feel the bright eyes *parallelism*
	  Of the beautiful Annabel Lee – *parallelism*
	And so, all the night-tide, I lie down by the side
	Of my darling —my darling—my life and my bride,
	  In her sepulchre there by the sea – *repetition*
	  In her tomb by the sounding sea. *He lies next to her body?!*
		The speaker dreams about Annabel Lee every night. He loves her so much he wants to be near her as much as possible. His obsession with her causes him to go to her tomb every night to sleep next to her.

113

TPCASTT Poetry Analysis

Poem Used:

T Title	
P Paraphrase	
C Connotation	
A Attitude	
S Shifts	
T Title Revisited	
T Theme	

TPCASTT Poetry Analysis

Poem Used:

T **Title**	**Title** What do you think the title of the poem means? Do you have any predictions about the poem?
P **Paraphrase**	**Paraphrase** Translate in your own words by line, stanza, or the overall poem. What is the poem about?
C **Connotation**	**Connotation** What meaning does the poem have beyond the literal meaning? Focus on such things as organizational pattern, diction, imagery, symbolism, literary devices, and other rhetorical devices.
A **Attitude**	**Attitude** What is the attitude of the author, speaker, and yourself?
S **Shifts**	**Shifts** Does the emotion or subject matter change? Is there a shift in tone, setting, voice, or structure? What is the purpose of each shift? How does it contribute to the meaning of the poem?
T **Title Revisited**	**Title Revisited** After having read the poem, does the title have any new meaning? Where your predictions about the poem correct? Would you add anything to your original meaning of the title?
T **Theme**	**Theme** What are the subjects and abstract ideas of the poem? What does the poem say about its subject? What overall statement is the poem making about life or humanity?

"The Wreck of the Hesperus"
By Henry Wadsworth Longfellow

Poem Stanza	Summary
It was the schooner *Hesperus,* That sailed the wint'ry sea; And the skipper had taken his little daughter, To bear him company.	
Blue were her eyes as the fairy-flax, Her cheeks like the dawn of day, And her bosom white as the hawthorn buds That ope in the month of May	
The skipper he stood beside the helm, His pipe was in his mouth, And he watched how the veering flaw did blow The smoke now West, now South.	
Then up and spake an old sailor, Had sailed the Spanish Main, "I pray thee put into yonder port, For I fear a hurricane.	
"Last night, the moon had a golden ring, And tonight no moon we see!" The skipper, he blew a whiff from his pipe, And a scornful laugh laughed he.	
Colder and louder blew the wind, A gale from the Northeast; The snow hissing in the brine, And the billows frothed like yeast.	
Down came the storm, and smote amain The vessel in its strength; She shuddered and paused, like a frighted steed, Then leaped her cable's length.	
"Come hither! Come hither! My little daughter, And do not tremble so; For I can weather the roughest gale That ever wind did blow."	
He wrapped her warm in his seaman's coat Against the stinging blast; He cut a rope from a broken spar, And bound her to the mast.	

Poem Stanza	Summary
"O father! I hear the church bells ring, O say what may it be?" "Tis a fog-bell on a rock-bound coast!" And he steered for the open sea.	
"O father! I hear the sound of guns, O say what may it be?" "Some ship in distress, that cannot live In such an angry sea!"	
"O father! I see a gleaming light, O say what may it be?" But the father answered never a word, A frozen corpse was he.	
Lashed to the helm, all stiff and stark, With his face turned to the skies, The lantern gleamed through the gleaming snow On his fixed and glassy eyes.	
Then the maiden clasped her hands and prayed That saved she might be; And she thought of Christ who stilled the wave On the Lake of Galilee.	
And fast through the midnight dark and drear, Through the whistling sleet and snow, Like a sheeted ghost, the vessel swept Towards the reef of Norman's Woe.	
And ever the fitful gusts between A sound came from the land; It was the sound of the trampling surf, On the rocks and the hard sea-sand.	
The breakers were right beneath her bows, She drifted a dreary wreck, And a whooping billow swept the crew Like icicles from her deck.	
She struck where the white and fleecy waves Looked soft as carded wool, But the cruel rocks, they gored her sides Like the horns of an angry bull.	

Poem Stanza	Summary
Her rattling shrouds, all sheathed in ice, With the masts went by the board; Like a vessel of glass she stove and sank, Ho! Ho! The breakers roared!	
At daybreak, on the bleak sea-beach, A fisherman stood aghast, To see the form of a maiden fair Lashed close to a drifting mast.	
The salt sea was frozen on her breast, The salt tears in her eyes; And he saw her hair, like the brown seaweed, On the billows fall and rise.	
Such was the wreck of the *Hesperus,* In the midnight and the snow! Christ save us all from a death like this On the reef of Norman's Woe!	

"The Wreck of the Hesperus"
Author's Craft/Purpose Questions

1. How does the description of the girl in the second stanza add to the sadness at the end of the poem?

2. What were some of the signs that a hurricane was coming?

3. What two things are the speaker comparing in stanza 7?

4. How did the skipper attempt to keep his daughter safe?

5. What happened to the skipper?

6. What is the purpose of the simile in the 17th stanza?

7. What is happening in the 18th stanza?

8. What does the word "aghast" mean in the 20th stanza?

9. What are some examples of visual imagery in the poem?

10. What is the theme of the poem?

TPCASTT Poetry Analysis
Answers

Poem Used: "The Wreck of the Hesperus" by Henry Wadsworth Longfellow

T **Title**	The word "wreck" has a negative connotation and indicates that something had an accident.
P **Paraphrase**	The poem is summarized by each stanza.
C **Connotation**	The speaker uses the similes, "Blue were her eyes as the fairy-flax, Her cheeks like to the dawn of day" to emphasize the girl's innocence. The simile, "She shuddered and paused, like a frighted steed" is used to accentuate the radical movements of the ship on the stormy sea. The speaker uses the Biblical allusion, "...Christ who stilled the wave on the Lake of Galilee" to show the girl's faith and desperation. The speaker uses the simile, "Like a sheeted ghost, the vessel swept" to establishes a negative and fearful connotation over what is happening with the ship. The imagery, "...her hair, like brown seaweed, on the billows fall and rise" creates a strong visual for readers to picture the innocent dead girl.
A **Attitude**	The speaker seems to have an attitude that it is the skipper's fault for bringing his daughter and not taking the storm warning seriously as evidenced by, "The skipper, he blew a whiff from his pipe, and a scornful laugh laughed he." The author creates a sympathetic feeling in the reader with the innocent descriptions of the girl versus the violent sea.
S **Shift**	There is a shift in the poem when the speaker describes, "Colder and louder blew the wind...the snow hissing in the brine..." to show that a serious storm is coming. There is another shift, "At daybreak...a fisherman stood aghast, to see the form of a maiden fair," which creates an eerie calm after the storm.
T **Title Revisited**	Looking back at the title after reading the poem, the reader has a much more personal and sad feeling about the Hesperus due to what happened to the crew and the innocent girl.
T **Theme**	The possible themes are: People should not take unnecessary chances, especially if loved ones are involved; Never underestimate the power of nature; Appreciate each day because you never know if it will be your last.

"The Wreck of the Hesperus"
Author's Craft/Purpose Questions Answers

1. How does the description of the girl in the second stanza add to the sadness at the end of the poem?
   The girl is portrayed as beautiful and innocent which makes it all the more sad that she died.

2. What were some of the signs that a hurricane was coming?
   The wind changed directions and they can't see the moon like they did the previous night.

3. What two things are the speaker comparing in stanza 7?
   The speaker is comparing the ship to a frightened steed the way it is moving.

4. How did the skipper attempt to keep his daughter safe?
   He took off his coat and put it on her and tied her to the mast so that she wouldn't be thrown overboard.

5. What happened to the skipper?
   The skipper froze to death because he was no longer wearing a coat.

6. What is the purpose of the simile in the 17th stanza?
   The description of the wind and waves shows how easily the men were tossed overboard.

7. What is happening in the 18th stanza?
   The wind and waves are forcing the ship into the shore and the rocks are tearing it apart.

8. What does the word "aghast" mean in the 20th stanza?
   Aghast means that the fisherman was shocked by the sight.

9. What are some examples of visual imagery in the poem?
   "And he saw her hair, like brown seaweed, on the billows fall and rise." Answers will vary.

10. What is the theme of the poem?
    The theme is that we shouldn't take unnecessary chances, especially when our loved ones are involved. It could also be that we can't underestimate the power of nature.

from *Sinners in the Hands of an Angry God*
by Jonathan Edwards

You probably are not sensible of this; you find you are kept out of hell, but do not see the hand of God in it; but look at other things, as the good state of your bodily constitution, your care of your own life, and the means you use for your own preservation. But indeed, these things are nothing; if God should withdraw His hand, they would avail no more to keep you from falling, than the thin air to hold up a person that is suspended in it.

Your wickedness makes it as you were heavy as lead, and to tend downwards with great weight and pressure towards hell; and if God should let you go, you would immediately sink and swiftly descend and plunge into the bottomless gulf, and your healthy constitution, and your own care and prudence, and best **contrivance**, and all your righteousness, would have no more influence to uphold you and keep you out of hell, than a spider's web would have to stop a fallen rock. Were it not for the sovereign pleasure of God, the earth would not bear you one moment; for you are a burden to it; the creation groans with you; the creature is made subject to the bondage of your corruption, not willingly; the sun does not willingly shine upon you to give you light to serve sin and Satan; the earth does not willingly yield her increase to satisfy your lusts; nor is it willingly a state for your wickedness to be acted upon; the air does not willingly serve you for breath to maintain the flame of life in your vitals, while you spend your life in the service of God's enemies. God's creatures are good, and were made for men to serve God with, and do not willingly **subserve** to any other purpose, and groan when they are abused to purposes so directly contrary to their nature and end. And the world would spew you out, were it not for the **sovereign** hand of Him who hath subjected it in hope. There are black clouds of God's wrath now hanging directly over your heads, full of the dreadful storm, and big with thunder; and were it not for the restraining hand of God, it would immediately burst forth upon you. The sovereign pleasure of God, for the present, stays His rough wind; otherwise, it would come with fury, and your destruction would come like a whirlwind, and you would be like the chaff of the summer threshing floor.

The bow of God's wrath is bent, and the arrow made ready on the string, and justice bends the arrow at your heart, and strains the bow, and it is nothing but the mere pleasure of God, and that of an angry God, without any promise or obligation at all, that keeps the arrow one moment from being made drunk with your blood. Thus, all you that never passed under a great change of heart by the mighty power of the Spirit of God upon your

souls, all you that were never born again, and made new creatures, and raised from being dead in sin, to a state of new, and before altogether unexperienced light and life, are in the hands of an angry God. However, you may have reformed your life in many things, and may have had religious affections, and may keep up a form of religious affections, and may keep up a form of religion in your families and closets, and in the house of God, it is nothing but His mere pleasure that keeps you from being this moment swallowed up in everlasting destruction. However unconvinced you may now be of the truth of what you hear, by and by you will be fully convinced of it. Those that are gone from being in the like circumstances with you see that it was so with them; for destruction came suddenly upon most of them; when they expected nothing of it and while they were saying, peace and safety; now they see that those things on which they depended for peace and safety, were nothing but thin air and empty shadows.

The God that holds you over the pit of hell, much as one holds a spider or some loathsome insect over the fire **abhors** you and is dreadfully provoked. His wrath towards you burns like fire; He looks upon you as worthy of nothing else but to be cast into the fire. He is of purer eyes than to bear to have you in His sight; you are ten thousand times more abominable in His eyes than the most hateful venomous serpent is in ours. You have offended Him infinitely more than ever a stubborn rebel did his prince; and yet it is nothing but His hand that holds you from falling into the fire every moment. It is to be ascribed to nothing else that you did not go to hell the last night; that you were suffered to awake again in this world, after you closed your eyes to sleep. And there is no other reason to be given why you have not dropped into hell since you arose in the morning, but that God's hand has held you up. There is no other reason to be given why you have not gone to hell, since you have sat here in the house of God, provoking His pure eyes by your sinful wicked manner of attending His solemn worship. Yea, there is nothing else that is to be given as a reason why you do not this very moment drop down into hell.

O sinner! Consider the fearful danger you are in it is a great furnace of wrath, a wide and bottomless pit, full of the fire of wrath, that you are held over in the hand of that God, whose wrath is provoked and incensed as much against you, as against you, as against many of the damned in hell. You hang by a slender thread, with the flames of divine wrath flashing about it, and ready every moment to singe it, and burn it **asunder**; and you have no interest in any Mediator, and nothing to lay hold of to save yourself, nothing to keep off the flames of wrath, nothing of your own, nothing that you have done, nothing that you can do, to induce God to spare you one moment.

"Sinners in the Hands of an Angry God"
Literary Device Identification Chart

Literary Device	Text Example	Author's Purpose
Simile		
Metaphor		
Personification		
Parallelism		
Imagery		

125

"Sinners in the Hands of an Angry God"
Vocabulary Identification Chart

Vocabulary Word	What I Think It Means (Using Context Clues)	Definition
Contrivance		
Subserve		
Sovereign		
Abhors		
Asunder		

© 2024 Rohach

126

"Sinners in the Hands of an Angry God"
Literary Device Identification Chart
Answers

Literary Device	Text Example	Author's Purpose
Simile	"The God that holds you over the pit of hell, much as one holds a spider or some loathsome insect over the fire, abhors you and is dreadfully provoked."	The author provides a visual comparing God's wrath to holding a spider to help people understand how fragile life is and how easily it can be taken away.
Metaphor	"There are black clouds of God's wrath now hanging directly over your heads, full of dreadful storm, and big with thunder…"	By comparing God's wrath to a familiar and threatening event, the author attempts to create additional fear in the parishioners.
Personification	"… the air does not willingly serve you for breath to maintain the flame of life in your vitals, while you spend your life in the service of God's enemies."	The author is pointing out that since we all require air to breath and exist, it is only because of God's mercy and not something we're entitled to.
Parallelism	"… now they see that those things on which they depended for peace and safety, were nothing but thin air and empty shadows."	The author uses parallelism to provide the reader with a pattern to simplify the explanation that the only thing we can truly count on is God.
Imagery	"The bow of God's wrath is bent, and the arrow made ready on the string … and it is nothing but the mere pleasure of God …that keeps the arrow one moment from being made drunk with your blood."	The author uses a vivid picture to convince parishioners that they should feel blessed and fortunate that God has extended mercy to them rather than enforcing his wrath.

"Sinners in the Hands of an Angry God"
Vocabulary Identification Chart
Answers

Vocabulary Word	What I Think It Means (Using Context Clues)	Definition
Contrivance	Answers will vary.	Contrivance is the act of intentionally arranging for something to happen by clever planning, or something that is arranged in this way.
Subserve	Answers will vary.	Subserve is subordination or instrumentally; to be subservient to; to help forward; to promote.
Sovereign	Answers will vary.	Sovereign is having supreme power or authority.
Abhors	Answers will vary.	Abhor means to regard with disgust and hatred.
Asunder	Answers will vary.	Asunder means being shattered or broken up into little pieces.

"Sinners in the Hands of an Angry God"
Famous American Evangelists Chart

There have been many American evangelists throughout history, and many have achieved fame for their personalities and/or messages. Below are five Americans who achieved fame as evangelists. Research each of the five to determine when they were at the height of their popularity and for what they are most famous.

American Evangelists	Applicable Dates	For What They Are Famous
Joel Osteen		
Billy Graham		
Cotton Mather		
Jimmy Swaggert		
Jim Bakker		

129

"Sinners in the Hands of an Angry God"
Famous American Evangelists Chart
Answers

There have been many American evangelists throughout history, and many have achieved fame for their personalities and/or messages. Below are five Americans who achieved fame as evangelists. Research each of the five to determine when they were at the height of their popularity and for what they are most famous.

American Evangelists	Applicable Dates	For What They Are Famous
Joel Osteen	1999-Present	He is famous for writing several books about finding strength within yourself and relying on God for help.
Billy Graham	1950-2018	He was well-known for his stellar reputation and his message that God forgives sins and offers salvation.
Cotton Mather	1680s-1728	He preached similarly to Jonathan Edwards and believed in a wrathful God. He also believed in witches.
Jimmy Swaggert	1980s	He was a popular television evangelist in the 1980's who was caught in a sex scandal involving prostitutes.
Jim Bakker	1970s-1980s	He and his wife, Tammy Faye, were extremely successful televangelists who co-founded the PTL club. He was caught cheating on his wife and received jail time for embezzlement.

Non-fiction Analysis Activity

1. Write specific examples and the significance of ethos, pathos, and logos used in the passage.

   Ethos –

   Pathos –

   Logos -

2. Write examples of significant diction that the author used and the purpose for it.

3. Discuss the significance of the syntax if applicable.

Strategy/Example from Text	Author's Purpose

4. Explain any significant shifts in the passage and the purpose of them.

5. Explain any logical fallacies used by the author and the purpose of them.

6. Based on the analysis, what was the author's message?

Non-fiction Analysis Activity

1. Read and annotate the passage to determine the author's purpose for the piece. Label all examples of **ethos**, **pathos**, and **logos**.

2. Divide the passage into sections and write a **summary** beside each section.

3. Identify any use of **irony**, **sarcasm**, or **motifs** and mark them as such.

4. Choose a color and highlight any significant **diction** which stands out for connotative or other reasons.

5. Underline unusual or significant **syntax**.

6. Choose an additional color and highlight literary devices such as: **antithesis**, **parallelism**, **anaphora**, **similes**, **metaphors**, etc. that you find in the passage.

7. Create a key for the colors you used.

8. Identify any **shifts** in the passage and mark them as such.

9. Put a box around **logical fallacies** used in the passage.

from *Narrative of the Life of Frederick Douglass, an American Slave*

If at any one time of my life more than another, I was made to drink the bitterest dregs of slavery, that time was during the first six months of my stay with Mr. Covey. We were worked in all weathers. It was never too hot or too cold; it could never rain, blow, hail, or snow, too hard for us to work in the field. Work, work, work, was scarcely more the order of the day than of the night. The longest days were too short for him, and the shortest nights were too long for him. I was somewhat unmanageable when I first went there, but a few months of this discipline tamed me. Mr. Covey succeeded in breaking me. I was broken in body, soul, and spirit. My natural elasticity was crushed, my intellect languished, the disposition to read departed, the cheerful spark that lingered about my eye died; the dark night of slavery closed in upon me; and behold a man transformed into a brute! .

Our house stood within a few rods of the Chesapeake Bay, whose broad bosom was ever white with sails from every quarter of the habitable globe. Those beautiful vessels, robed in purest white, so delightful to the eye of freemen, were to me so many shrouded ghosts, to terrify and torment me with thoughts of my wretched condition. I have often, in the deep stillness of a summer's Sabbath, stood all alone upon the lofty banks of that noble bay, and traced, with saddened heart and tearful eye, the countless number of sails moving off to the mighty ocean. The sight of these always affected me powerfully. My thoughts would compel utterance; and there, with no audience but the Almighty, I would pour out my soul's complaint, in my rude way, with an apostrophe to the moving multitude of ships: --

"You are loosed from your moorings, and are free; and I am fast in my chains, and am a slave! You move merrily before the gentle gale, and I sadly before the bloody whip! You are freedom's swift-winged angels, that fly round the world; I am confined in bands of iron! O that I were free! O, that I were on one of your gallant decks, and under your protecting wing! Alas! Betwixt me and you, the turbid waters roll. Go on, go on. O that I could also go! Could I but swim! If I could fly! O, why was I born a man, of whom to make a brute! The glad ship is gone; she hides in the dim distance. I am left in the hottest hell of unending slavery. O God, save me! God deliver me! Let me be free! Is there any God? Why am I a slave? I will run away. I will not stand it. Get caught or get clear, I'll try it. I had as well die with ague as the fever. I have only one life to lose. I had as well be killed running as die standing. Only think of it; one hundred miles straight north, and I am free! Try it? Yes! God helping me, I will. It cannot be that I shall live and die a slave. I will take to the water. This very bay shall bear me into freedom. The steamboats steered in a north-east course from North Point. I will do the same; and when I get to the head of the bay, I will turn my canoe adrift, and walk straight through Delaware into Pennsylvania. When I get there, I shall not be required to have a pass; I can travel without being disturbed. Let but the first opportunity offer, and, come what will, I am off. Meanwhile, I will try to bear up under the yoke. I am not the only slave in the world. Why should I fret? I can bear as much as any of them. Besides, I am but a boy, and all boys are bound to someone. It may be that my misery in slavery will only increase my happiness when I get free. There is a better day coming."

Thus I used to think, and thus I used to speak to myself; goaded almost to madness at one moment, and at the next reconciling myself to my wretched lot.

Narrative of the Life of Frederick Douglass Appendix
Author's Craft for Author's
Purpose Chart

Literary Device	Example from Text	Purpose of Device
Parallelism		
Anaphora		
Juxtaposition		

Author's Message/Purpose:

from *Narrative of the Life of Frederick Douglass, an American Slave*

If at any one time of my life more than another, I was made to drink the bitterest dregs of slavery, that time was during the first six months of my stay with Mr. Covey. We were worked in all weathers. It was never too hot or too cold; it could never rain, blow, hail, or snow, too hard for us to work in the field. Work, work, work, was scarcely more the order of the day than of the night. The longest days were too short for him, and the shortest nights were too long for him. I was somewhat unmanageable when I first went there, but a few months of this discipline tamed me. Mr. Covey succeeded in breaking me. I was broken in body, soul, and spirit. My natural elasticity was crushed, my intellect languished, the disposition to read departed, the cheerful spark that lingered about my eye died; the dark night of slavery closed in upon me; and behold a man transformed into a brute! ...

Our house stood within a few rods of the Chesapeake Bay, whose broad bosom was ever white with sails from every quarter of the habitable globe. Those beautiful vessels, robed in purest white, so delightful to the eye of freemen, were to me so many shrouded ghosts, to terrify and torment me with thoughts of my wretched condition. I have often, in the deep stillness of a summer's Sabbath, stood all alone upon the lofty banks of that noble bay, and traced, with saddened heart and tearful eye, the countless number of sails moving off to the mighty ocean. The sight of these always affected me powerfully. My thoughts would compel utterance; and there, with no audience but the Almighty, I would pour out my soul's complaint, in my rude way, with an apostrophe to the moving multitude of ships: --

"You are loosed from your moorings, and are free; and I am fast in my chains, and am a slave! You move merrily before the gentle gale, and I sadly before the bloody whip! You are freedom's swift-winged angels, that fly round the world; I am confined in bands of iron! O that I were free! O, that I were on one of your gallant decks, and under your protecting wing! Alas! Betwixt me and you, the turbid waters roll. Go on, go on. O that I could also go! Could I but swim! If I could fly! O, why was I born a man, of whom to make a brute! The glad ship is gone; she hides in the dim distance. I am left in the hottest hell of unending slavery. O God, save me! God deliver me! Let me be free! Is there any God? Why am I a slave? I will run away. I will not stand it. Get caught or get clear, I'll try it. I had as well die with ague as the fever. I have only one life to lose. I had as well be killed running as die standing. Only think of it; one hundred miles straight north, and I am free! Try it? Yes! God helping me, I will. It cannot be that I shall live and die a slave. I will take to the water. This very bay shall bear me into freedom. The steamboats steered in a north-east course from North Point. I will do the same; and when I get to the head of the bay, I will turn my canoe adrift, and walk straight through Delaware into Pennsylvania. When I get there, I shall not be required to have a pass; I can travel without being disturbed. Let but the first opportunity offer, and, come what will, I am off. Meanwhile, I will try to bear up under the yoke. I am not the only slave in the world. Why should I fret? I can bear as much as any of them. Besides, I am but a boy, and all boys are bound to someone. It may be that my misery in slavery will only increase my happiness when I get free. There is a better day coming."

Thus I used to think, and thus I used to speak to myself; goaded almost to madness at one moment, and at the next reconciling myself to my wretched lot.

[Handwritten margin annotations:]
- Douglass describes the evil nature of the slave master.
- Douglass describes the beauty of the bay where he lived.
- Douglass describes the torment and frustration of watching the ships sail freely while he was in bondage.
- Shift
- Douglass again resigns himself to the fact that he will most likely always be a slave.

[Handwritten literary device labels:] antithesis, parallelism, repetition, antithesis, Pathos, personification, metaphor, antithesis, Logos, metaphor, Pathos, anaphora, parallelism, personification, antithesis, anaphora, Logos

Narrative of the Life of Frederick Douglass Appendix
Author's Craft for Author's
Purpose Chart Answers

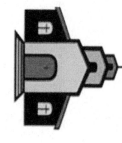

Literary Device	Example from Text	Purpose of Device
Parallelism	"Good, pure, holy," "bad, corrupt, and wicked," "the climax of all misnomers, the boldest of all frauds, and the grossest of all libels."	Douglass uses this device to show the consistency with which people claim to be Christians while mistreating and using slaves.
Anaphora	"He who…," "The man who…"	Anaphora is used to boldly point out those who act as authority on Christ and God's laws but do the exact opposite of what they preach.
Juxtaposition	"The slave auctioneer's bell and the church-going bell," "bitter cries…religious shouts"	Douglass juxtaposes the way he sees Christianity as opposed to the way other supposed Christians perceive it.

Author's Message/Purpose:

People who own slaves or support those who do while claiming to be Christians are hypocrites and living a life of deceit.

Introduction for Analysis

Title	
Author	
Genre	
Background/ Audience	
Purpose	
Strategies	

Introduction:_____

_____

_____

_____

_____

Narrative of the Life of Frederick Douglass
Introduction for Rhetorical Analysis Answers

Title	*Narrative of the Life of Frederick Douglass* Appendix
Author	Frederick Douglass
Genre	Autobiography
Background/ Audience	Frederick Douglass was a slave who taught himself to read, escaped, and became an activist.
Purpose	The purpose of the excerpt was to exemplify the hypocrisy of slave holders who claimed to be Christians.
Strategies	The strategies used were parallelism, anaphora, and juxtaposition.

Introduction:

In the appendix to his autobiography, *Narrative of the Life of Frederick Douglass,* Douglass attempts to clarify his beliefs about Christianity by pointing out the hypocrisy of slaveowners and their Christian beliefs. He used parallelism, anaphora, and juxtaposition to explain his resentment.

Comprehending Non-fiction

Text Used: _____

Main Idea	
What is the main idea of each page/section/chapter?	What is the main idea of the selection?

Key Details	
What are the details in the text which support the main idea?	Compare and contrast key details in the text.

Vocabulary or Rhetorical Devices

Meaningful Word or Rhetorical Device	Author's Purpose

Text Features

What are significant, subtitles, headings, graphics, pictures, or graphs?	What is the meaning of each text feature?

 SOAPSTONE Analysis

Text Used_____

S	Speaker	
O	Occasion	
A	Audience	
P	Purpose	
S	Subject	
Tone		

SOAPSTONE Analysis

Speaker – Who is the Speaker?

The voice that tells the story is the speaker. When students approach a text, they often believe that the author and the speaker of the piece are the same. This assumption is not necessarily sound. In fiction, the author may choose to tell the story through the words in any number of different kinds of characters. Even nonfiction writers may use points of view that conceal or alter their actual beliefs or opinions. These points of view do not make the text any less valid, but they do require readers to interpret each voice.

Thus, before students begin to write they must decide whose voice is going to be heard. Whether this voice belongs to a fictional character or to the writers themselves, students should determine how the various attributes of the speaker will influence the perceived meaning of the piece.

Occasion – What is the Occasion?

The occasion is the time and place of the piece or the context that prompted the writing to occur. There is the larger occasion: an environment of ideas and emotions that swirl around a broad issue. Then there is the immediate occasion: an event or situation that catches the writer's attention and triggers a response. Readers must place themselves with this context so that they understand the writer's motivation for creating the text.

Audience – Who is the Audience?

Audience is the group of readers to whom this piece is directed. As they begin to write, students must determine who the audience is that they intend to address. It may be one person or a specific group. This choice of audience will affect how and why students write a particular text.

Purpose – What is the Purpose?

Purpose is the reason behind the text. Students need to consider the purpose of the text in order to develop the argument and its logic. They should ask themselves this question: "What do I want my audience to think or do as a result of reading my text?"

Subject – What is the Subject?

The subject is the general topic, content, and ideas contained in the text. Students should be able to state the subject in a few words or a phrase. This technique helps students focus on the task throughout the writing process.

TONE – What is the Tone?

The attitude of the author is the tone. The spoken word can convey the speaker's attitude and thus help to impart meaning through tone of voice. With the written word, it is tone that extends meaning beyond the literal, and students must learn to convey this tone in their diction (choice of words), syntax (sentence construction), and imagery (metaphors, similes, and other types of figurative language.) The ability to manage tone is one of the best indicators of a writer's sophistication.

from *Narrative of the Life of Frederick Douglass, an American Slave*

If at any one time of my life more than another, I was made to drink the bitterest dregs of slavery, that time was during the first six months of my stay with Mr. Covey. We were worked in all weathers. It was never too hot or too cold; it could never rain, blow, hail, or snow, too hard for us to work in the field. Work, work, work, was scarcely more the order of the day than of the night. The longest days were too short for him, and the shortest nights were too long for him. I was somewhat unmanageable when I first went there, but a few months of this discipline tamed me. Mr. Covey succeeded in breaking me. I was broken in body, soul, and spirit. My natural elasticity was crushed, my intellect languished, the disposition to read departed, the cheerful spark that lingered about my eye died; the dark night of slavery closed in upon me; and behold a man transformed into a brute!

Our house stood within a few rods of the Chesapeake Bay, whose broad bosom was ever white with sails from every quarter of the habitable globe. Those beautiful vessels, robed in purest white, so delightful to the eye of freemen, were to me so many shrouded ghosts, to terrify and torment me with thoughts of my wretched condition. I have often, in the deep stillness of a summer's Sabbath, stood all alone upon the lofty banks of that noble bay, and traced, with saddened heart and tearful eye, the countless number of sails moving off to the mighty ocean. The sight of these always affected me powerfully. My thoughts would compel utterance; and there, with no audience but the Almighty, I would pour out my soul's complaint, in my rude way, with an apostrophe to the moving multitude of ships: --

"You are loosed from your moorings, and are free; and I am fast in my chains, and am a slave! You move merrily before the gentle gale, and I sadly before the bloody whip! You are freedom's swift-winged angels, that fly round the world; I am confined in bands of iron! O that I were free! O, that I were on one of your gallant decks, and under your protecting wing! Alas! Betwixt me and you, the turbid waters roll. Go on, go on. O that I could also go! Could I but swim! If I could fly! O, why was I born a man, of whom to make a brute! The glad ship is gone; she hides in the dim distance. I am left in the hottest hell of unending slavery. O God, save me! God deliver me! Let me be free! Is there any God? Why am I a slave? I will run away. I will not stand it. Get caught or get clear, I'll try it. I had as well die with ague as the fever. I have only one life to lose. I had as well be killed running as die standing. Only think of it; one hundred miles straight north, and I am free! Try it? Yes! God helping me, I will. It cannot be that I shall live and die a slave. I will take to the water. This very bay shall bear me into freedom. The steamboats steered in a north-east course from North Point. I will do the same; and when I get to the head of the bay, I will turn my canoe adrift, and walk straight through Delaware into Pennsylvania. When I get there, I shall not be required to have a pass; I can travel without being disturbed. Let but the first opportunity offer, and, come what will, I am off. Meanwhile, I will try to bear up under the yoke. I am not the only slave in the world. Why should I fret? I can bear as much as any of them. Besides, I am but a boy, and all boys are bound to someone. It may be that my misery in slavery will only increase my happiness when I get free. There is a better day coming."

Thus I used to think, and thus I used to speak to myself; goaded almost to madness at one moment, and at the next reconciling myself to my wretched lot.

SOAPSTONE Analysis
Answers

Text Used: Passage from *Narrative of the Life of Frederick Douglass*

S	Speaker	The speaker in the passage is Frederick Douglass who is looking back at a certain time in his life.
O	Occasion	The occasion was a time in Douglass's life as a slave when he lived on Chesapeake Bay and watched the ships sailing freely. This caused him to long for the freedom that the ships had.
A	Audience	Douglass was speaking to free men who had never experienced the evils of slavery.
P	Purpose	Douglass's purpose was to accurately portray the true cruelty and inhumanity of slavey on a person.
S	Subject	The subject was what the implications of being enslaved does to a person's psyche.
Tone		Throughout this passage, Douglass's tone changed from defeat, to anger, to urgency and desperation, and finally to reluctant acceptance.

Get a Clue
Vocabulary in Context

Word in Context	What I Think the Word Means	Dictionary Definition

Plot Diagram

What is the Title? _____

Who is the Author? _____

Who are the Characters? _____

Who is the Protagonist? _____

Who is the Antagonist? _____

Climax
Peak Moment

Rising Action
What is the struggle?

Falling Action

Exposition/Base

Resolution
What is the Solution?

What is the Setting?

What is the Theme?

Rolling for Reading Strategies

In groups of 3 or 4, have each person roll a die to respond to the corresponding reading strategy.

Diction/Connotation – The following words in the selection: _____ and _____ create a feeling of _____.

Details – The most important detail in the paragraph/story or stanza/poem is _____ **because** _____.

Setting – The setting of the selection _____ **is important because** _____.

Connections – This story makes me think of the following personal/historical/societal event because _____.

Vocabulary – The following word, _____, **was difficult to understand, but I now know that it means** _____.

The author's message in this selection is _____. **I know this because** _____.

MAKING A MOVIE USING THE PLOT DIAGRAM

Using the reading selection, identify the parts of the plot and wrie a summary or illustrate each in the correct box.

Title of Story _____

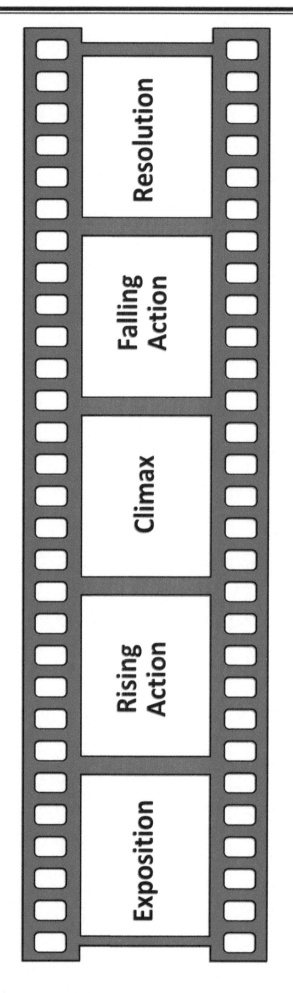

Read for Three

CONTENT

Read the selection for understanding. What does the text say? What is happening in the selection?

CLARITY

Read the selection for meaning. What events, characters, or ideas stand out in the selection?

CONCEPTION

Read the selection to determine the message. What strategies did the author use to convey his message?

Could Be, Can't Be, Probably

Read the question and label each answer as:

Could Be (—)
Can't Be (X)
Probably (+)

Write a short explanation for each.

Get in a group of 2-4 and compare answers. If everyone has an X by the same answer, draw a line through that answer.

If everyone has a (+) by the same answer, highlight that answer and read what each person wrote as why it was the correct answer.

If everyone doesn't have a (+) by the same answer, read what each person wrote for each of the (--) answers and determine as a group which answer is the correct one.

Text the Tale

Use text messages to summarize events in the story. Determine which character's message is in the dark and which is in the light. Write the text beside the phone.

Character in Dark Text: _____

Character in Light Text: _____

SECTION THREE

WRITING

"Don't tell me the moon is shining; show me the glint of light on broken glass."

Anton Chekhov

TAPE Strategy
Tackling SCRs
Short Constructed Response Questions

T	**Think**	What is the question actually asking? Do I have more than one choice for an answer? Which answer has the best evidence for me to use?
A	**Answer**	Answer the question clearly in complete sentences.
P	**Prove**	Provide textual proof that the answer you stated is correct.
E	**Elaborate**	Elaborate and add details to show your knowledge of the text. Make sure that you stay on topic and answer the question completely.

SCR Answer

TAPE Strategy
Tackling SCRs
Short Constructed Response Questions

T	
A	
P	
E	

SCR Answer

from *Narrative of the Life of Frederick Douglass, an American Slave*

If at any one time of my life more than another, I was made to drink the bitterest dregs of slavery, that time was during the first six months of my stay with Mr. Covey. We were worked in all weathers. It was never too hot or too cold; it could never rain, blow, hail, or snow, too hard for us to work in the field. Work, work, work, was scarcely more the order of the day than of the night. The longest days were too short for him, and the shortest nights were too long for him. I was somewhat unmanageable when I first went there, but a few months of this discipline tamed me. Mr. Covey succeeded in breaking me. I was broken in body, soul, and spirit. My natural elasticity was crushed, my intellect languished, the disposition to read departed, the cheerful spark that lingered about my eye died; the dark night of slavery closed in upon me; and behold a man transformed into a brute!

Our house stood within a few rods of the Chesapeake Bay, whose broad bosom was ever white with sails from every quarter of the habitable globe. Those beautiful vessels, robed in purest white, so delightful to the eye of freemen, were to me so many shrouded ghosts, to terrify and torment me with thoughts of my wretched condition. I have often, in the deep stillness of a summer's Sabbath, stood all alone upon the lofty banks of that noble bay, and traced, with saddened heart and tearful eye, the countless number of sails moving off to the mighty ocean. The sight of these always affected me powerfully. My thoughts would compel utterance; and there, with no audience but the Almighty, I would pour out my soul's complaint, in my rude way, with an apostrophe to the moving multitude of ships:

"You are loosed from your moorings and are free; and I am fast in my chains and am a slave! You move merrily before the gentle gale, and I sadly before the bloody whip! You are freedom's swift-winged angels, that fly round the world; I am confined in bands of iron! O that I were free! O, that I were on one of your gallant decks, and under your protecting wing! Alas! Betwixt me and you, the turbid waters roll. Go on, go on. O that I could also go! Could I but swim! If I could fly! O, why was I born a man, of whom to make a brute! The glad ship is gone; she hides in the dim distance. I am left in the hottest hell of unending slavery. O God, save me! God deliver me! Let me be free! Is there any God? Why am I a slave? I will run away. I will not stand it. Get caught or get clear, I'll try it. I had as well die with ague as the fever. I have only one life to lose. I had as well be killed running as die standing. Only think of it; one hundred miles straight north, and I am free! Try it? Yes! God helping me, I will. It cannot be that I shall live and die a slave. I will take to the water. This very bay shall bear me into freedom. The steamboats steered in a north-east course from North Point. I will do the same; and when I get to the head of the bay, I will turn my canoe adrift, and walk straight through Delaware into Pennsylvania. When I get there, I shall not be required to have a pass; I can travel without being disturbed. Let but the first opportunity offer, and, come what will, I am off. Meanwhile, I will try to bear up under the yoke. I am not the only slave in the world. Why should I fret? I can bear as much as any of them. Besides, I am but a boy, and all boys are bound to someone. It may be that my misery in slavery will only increase my happiness when I get free. There is a better day coming."

Thus, I used to think, and thus I used to speak to myself; goaded almost to madness at one moment, and at the next reconciling myself to my wretched lot.

SCR Question

Read the following sentence from the passage.

> You are freedom's swift-winged angels that fly around the world.

How does the metaphor accurately emphasize the author's viewpoint about slavery? Support your answer with evidence from the selection.

TAPE Strategy
Tackling SCRs
Short Constructed Response Questions
Answers

T	This metaphor is talking about the ships and how they are free to sail the ocean, but he is a man and not free to move about as he pleases. This reinforces his viewpoint that slavery is absurd and adds to his frustration.
A	This metaphor describing the freedom of the ship's movements shows how frustrated Douglass is that he does not have the same freedom to move about.
P	"You are loosed from your moorings and are free; I am fast in my chains and am a slave!"
E	Douglass is tortured by having to watch the movement of the ships in the bay knowing that he does not have the same freedom as these manmade objects.

SCR Answer

This metaphor describing the freedom of the ship's movements shows how frustrated Douglass is that he does not have the same freedom to move about. The quote, "You are loosed from your moorings and are free; I am fast in my chains and am a slave!" shows Douglass's extreme exasperation. Douglass finds absurdity in slavery and is tortured by having to watch the movement of the ships in the bay knowing that he does not have the same freedom as these manmade objects.

Thesis Statement Activity

A **<u>thesis statement</u>** is one complete sentence which narrows the topic down to a specific focus of you investigation. It must contain an **<u>opinion</u>** which the writer intends to prove. **A thesis statement is not a statement of fact.**

Thesis Statement: Smoking is a disgusting habit which impedes the freedom of others.

Not a Thesis Statement: Smoking has been proven to cause cancer and other health-related issues in individuals. (This is a detail which is also a fact; therefore, it cannot be a thesis statement because there is no need to prove it.)

Step 1. Read articles highlighting major ideas about your topic while keeping in mind **your position on your topic**.

Step 2. Find major ideas within your sources that **support your position on your topic**. In your own words and using complete sentences, list the reasons or supporting facts about your topic.

These will become the main points in your outline.

1. _____

2. _____

3. _____

4. _____

5. _____

Step 3. Write a statement about your topic which takes a stand and justifies further discussion. Be sure not to use the words "I think" or "I believe" because this will weaken your argument.

This will be your working **thesis statement**.

_____

_____

_____

_____

Steps of the Persuasive Essay

Write an essay explaining whether or not talking to people is more important than communicating by phone. (Pretend that we are having an argument and it is important that you prove to me that you are right.)

Planning (List reasons on both sides).

Talking   Texting

_____   _____

_____   _____

_____   _____

_____   _____

Choose the side with the strongest reasons and circle the best one.

Introduction (Turn the questions into a statement and add "because" and the reason you circled.)

(Talking or texting) is more important because _____

_____.

Body (Remember that you are trying to prove a point. You will not win the argument if you give weak examples.)

- Example 1: State a specific example from a history, entertainment, literature (movies), personal example, etc. (HELP)
- Example 2: State another specific example.

Counterargument and Rebuttal (State the opposition and why their reasoning is flawed.)

Although some people feel that _____(opposing reason)_____is more important because _____, in reality _(my idea)_ is better because (why opposing view is a bad idea).

Conclusion (Restate the introduction using different words.)

It is important that _____ because _____.

$15 Minimum Wage
Ethos, Pathos, Logos Activity Directions

1. Divide the class into groups of two, three, or four.

2. Make several copies of the activity page.

3. Cut out each of the squares so that it looks like the example below:

4. Give each group a copy of each of the squares.

5. Have the students write in the top box whether it is primarily **Ethos**, **Pathos**, or **Logos**.

6. Sort the examples by putting them in the proper column according to whether they are a **PRO** or a **CON** argument.

7. Check and make sure each group has sorted them correctly.

8. Once they have correctly completed the sorting, have each group write a pro and a con example and tell whether each is ethos, pathos, or logos.

$15 Minimum Wage
Ethos, Pathos, Logos Activity Answers

PRO (FOR)	CON (AGAINST)

Ethos

This country has a duty to take care of its citizens and lower the number of people living in poverty.

Ethos

People have a responsibility to acquire the amount of experience or education that is required to get a higher paying job.

Pathos

Single mothers need the extra money to be able to take care of their families.

Pathos

Small businesses can't afford to pay more money to their workers and will have to close.

Logos

If we don't do something about those living in poverty, the homeless population will continue to increase.

Logos

If we raise the minimum wage, prices will be affected, and it will be harmful to everyone including those it is meant to help.

$15 Minimum Wage
Ethos, Pathos, Logos Activity

PRO (FOR)	CON (AGAINST)
This country has a duty to take care of its citizens and lower the number of people living in poverty.	People have a responsibility to acquire the amount of experience or education that is required to get a higher paying job.
Single mothers need the extra money to be able to take care of their families.	Small businesses can't afford to pay more money to their workers and will have to close.
If we don't do something about those living in poverty, the homeless population will continue to increase.	If we raise the minimum raise, prices will be affected, and it will be harmful to everyone including those it is meant to help.

Parts of a Strong ARGUMENT

CLAIM = Statement the writer is trying to prove is true

Argument = The reason wich supports the claim

Evidence = Proof from a credible source; facts

Explanation = Explains what the evidence proves

Rationale = What the evidence and explanation show about the claim

COUNTERCLAIM
The statement opposing the claim; the other side

REBUTTAL
A reason why the counterclaim is not as strong as the claim

Conclusion = Restate the claim, summarize the argument, and make a recommendation

185

© 2024 Rohach

CLAIM =

Argument =

Evidence =

Explanation =

Rationale =

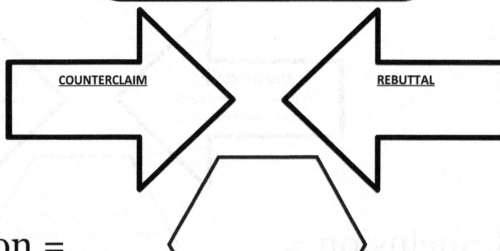

COUNTERCLAIM

REBUTTAL

Conclusion =

Instructions for Argument Activity

1. Divide the class into groups of two, three, or four.

2. Make sure that each group has a copy of the Statements of an Argument page.

3. Cut the page into strips of paper and mix them up.

4. Cut strips of paper from the Statements of an Argument page and make enough sets so that each group has one.

5. Give each student a copy of the chart.

6. Discuss each part and how it contributes to the argument.

7. Have groups read the strips of paper and put them in the proper place on the chart.

8. Make sure that each group has correctly filled out the argument chart.

9. Have students create their own statements from the opposing side of the argument and fill in the chart.

*You may choose to use a Carousel Activity in which you put up chart paper and have the students walk around the room attaching the statements to the correct parts of the argument.

Parts of a Strong ARGUMENT Answer

CLAIM =

Raising the minimum wage to $15 per hour is critical for the future benefit of our country.

Argument =

If the minimum wage for unskilled workers were increased to $15, the number of people living on welfare would dramaticall decrease.

Evidence =

Making the current minimum wage of $7.25 an hour is not enough maney for a simple mother to support her children without assistance.

Explanation =

The amount of money minimum wage workers are making is not rising as fast as the cost of living (gas, food, housing, electricity, water, etc.)

Rationale =

The logical conclusion is that the minimum wage should be raised to cover the cost of living so that people do not have to live in poverty and depend on government for assistance.

COUNTERCLAIM
If people don't wat to live in poverty and depend on government assistance, they should get a better education.

REBUTTAL
Not everyone has an equal opportunity or ability to get an education, so they need fair wages to be able to survive.

Conclusion =

The United States currently has far too many people living in poverty and depending on the government to survive due to circumstances beyond their control, so raising the minimum wage to $15 is a necessary solution.

Statements for the Argument

Raising the minimum wage to $15 per hour is critical for the future benefit of our country.
If the minimum wage for unskilled workers were increased to $15.00, the number of people living on welfare would dramatically decrease.
Making the current minimum wage of $7.25 an hour is not enough money for a single mother to support her children without government assistance.
The amount of money minimum wage workers are making is not rising as fast as the cost of living (gas, food, housing, electricity, water, etc.)
The logical conclusion is that the minimum wage should be raised to cover the cost of living so that people do not have to live in poverty and depend on the government for assistance.
If people don't want to live in poverty and depend on government assistance, they should get a better education.
Not everyone has an equal opportunity or ability to get an education, so they need fair wages to be able to survive.
The United States currently has far too many people living in poverty and depending on the government to survive due to circumstances beyond their control, so raising the minimum wage to $15.00 is a necessary solution.

Descriptive Organizational Pattern

(The purpose is to describe someone or something so a picture forms in the reader's mind.)

Passage Name: _____

Signal/Transition Words:

for example   in addition
for instance   such as
characteristics   is like
specifically   to illustrate

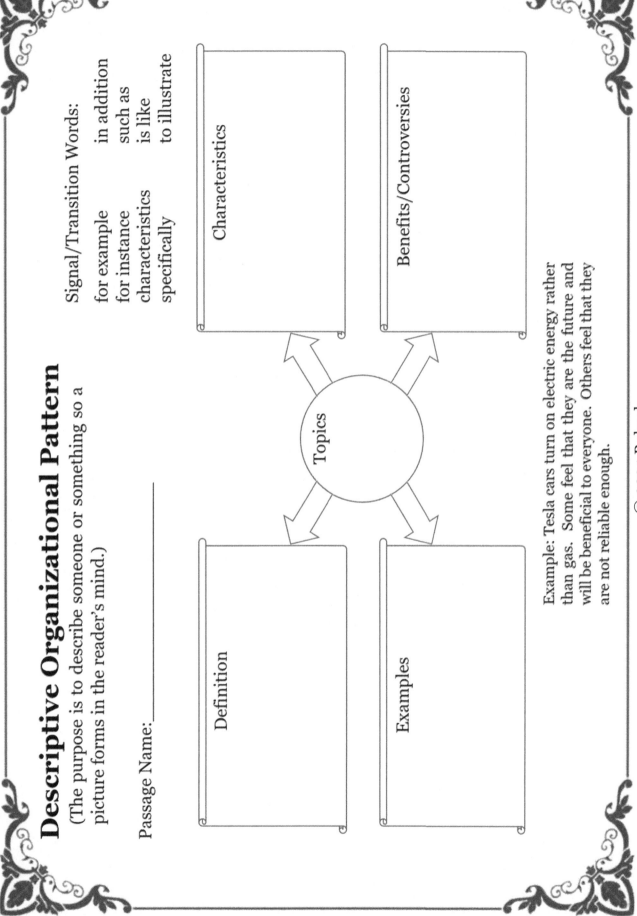

Definition

Examples

Topics

Characteristics

Benefits/Controversies

Example: Tesla cars turn on electric energy rather than gas. Some feel that they are the future and will be beneficial to everyone. Others feel that they are not reliable enough.

Compare and Contrast Organizational Pattern

(The purpose to compare the similarities and differences between two topics.)

Passage Name: _____

Example: All new cars have similar safety features such as seat belts and air bags; however, some new cars have additional safety features such as cameras and warning signals.

Signal/Transition Words

<u>compare</u>	<u>contrast</u>
similarly	but
likewise	although
as well	yet
too	however
in common	except
	on the contrary

What is being compared and contrasted?

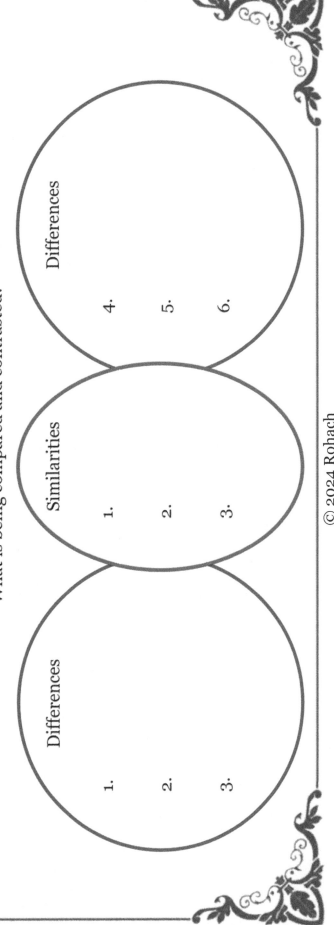

Differences
1.
2.
3.

Similarities
1.
2.
3.

Differences
4.
5.
6.

© 2024 Rohach

Chronological Organizational Pattern

(The purpose is to show the order in which something happens.)

Passage Name: _____

Example: When Jack first decided to drink alcohol, he did not know the risks of drinking. Over time, drinking slowly took control of his life. He eventually had a car accident which ended the life of a young woman.

Signal/Transition Words

first, second, third   while
soon, then, next   when
now, immediately   last, finally
until   before, during, after

Third Event

Most Recent Point in Time

Second Event

First Event

Earliest Point In Time

© 2024 Rohach

Cause and Effect Organization Pattern

(The purpose is to show how one event causes another event.)

Signal/Transition Words

for	since	thereby
because	due to	leads to
if, then	as a result	

Passage Name: _____

Example: It was snowing this morning, so I missed the bus; therefore, I could not take the final exam.

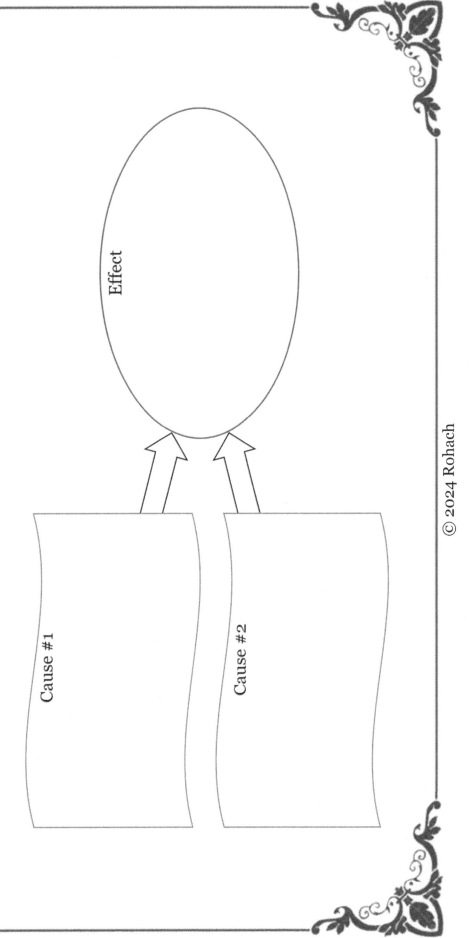

Effect

Cause #1

Cause #2

Problem and Solution Organizational Pattern

(The purpose is to outline a solution to a problem.)

Passage Name: _____

Example: Texting while driving is the number one killer of teens today. One solution is to use devices which disable phones when the car is running.

Signal/Transition Words

dilemma, problem   question is
to solve   one answer
solution   recommend
where this   one reason

Problem

Solution

Solution

Sequence Organizational Pattern

(The purpose is to show the order in which something happens.)

Signal/Transition Words

first, second, third   while
soon, then, next   when
now, immediately   last, finally
until   before, during, after

Passage Name: _____

1

2

3

4

Advantages and Disadvantages Organizational Pattern

(The purpose is to compare the advantages and disadvantages of a single topic.)

Passage Name: _____

Example: Tesla cars have advantages such as not using gas and saving the environment; however, they can only go as far as a charge will allow.

Signal/Transition Words

Compare	Contrast
similarly	but
likewise	although
as well	yet
too	however
in common	except
	on the contrary

What is the topic? _____

Advantages

1.

2.

3.

Disadvantages

1.

2.

3.

Organizational Patterns Review Lesson

Create a foldable by taking a sheet of paper and folding it in half hotdog style. Take the top piece of paper and make cuts to create six pieces. On each of the six pieces write one of the following: Compare and Contrast, Spatial, Chronological, Problem and Solution, Cause and Effect, and Sequence.

On the back of each piece have students write the definition of the pattern.

Cause and Effect – This pattern discusses a relationship between events or things where one is the result of the other.

Problem and Solution – This pattern discusses a difficulty and provides an answer.

Compare and Contrast – This pattern discusses the similarities and differences between two things.

Chronological – This pattern organizes information in order of time.

Spatial/Descriptive – This pattern describes how something looks or how it is arranged.

Sequence - a particular order in which related events, movements, or things follow each other.

On the second half of the folded paper, underneath each flap, have students draw the example of each pattern.

Cause and Effect	Problem/Solution	Compare/Contrast
Chronological	Spatial/Descriptive	Sequence

Compare/Contrast		Sequence	
Problem/Solution		Spatial/Descriptive	
Cause and Effect		Chronological	

Compare/Contrast	Problem/Solution	Cause and Effect
Sequence	Spatial/Descriptive	Chronological

Organizational Pattern Test

Choose the correct definition for each organizational pattern.

_____ 1. Cause and Effect

_____ 2. Problem/Solution

_____ 3. Compare/Contrast

_____ 4. Chronological

_____ 5. Spatial/Description

_____ 6. Sequence

A. This pattern discusses the similarities and differences between two things.

B. This pattern describes how something looks or how it is arranged.

C. This pattern organizes information in order of time.

D. This pattern discusses a difficulty and provides and answer.

E. This pattern discusses a relationship between events or things where one is the result of the other.

F. This pattern follows a particular order in which related events, movements, or things follow each other.

Identify the text structure in each passage.

7. _____ Kim's room is very large and overlooks the backyard. She has her own closet and her own bathroom. Her brother's room, on the other hand, is fairly small. Though her older brother was given first choice of rooms, he chose the smaller room because it felt cozier. His room has a smaller closet, no private bathroom, and overlooks the front yard.

8. _____ The walls in Kim's room are bright yellow. She has posters on the walls and striped, yellow curtains. Her bedspread is yellow and green.

9. _____ Kim has a system when it comes to cleaning her room. First, she picks up all her toys and puts them away. Then, she makes up her bed. Finally, she dusts and runs the vacuum cleaner.

10. _____ Kim's dad got offered a new job in a big, new city. It was a very good job with a very good salary, so her family moved over the summer.

Organizational Pattern Test   Answers

Choose the correct definition for each organizational pattern.

Identify the text structure in each passage.

_E_ 1. Cause and Effect

_D_ 2. Problem/Solution

_A_ 3. Compare/Contrast

_C_ 4. Chronological

_F_ 5. Spatial/Description

_B_ 6. Sequence

A. This pattern discusses the similarities and differences between two things.

B. This pattern describes how something looks or how it is arranged.

C. This pattern organizes information in order of time.

D. This pattern discusses a difficulty and provides and answer.

E. This pattern discusses a relationship between events or things where one is the result of the other.

F. This pattern follows a particular order in which related events, movements, or things follow each other.

7. **Compare/Contrast** Kim's room is very large and overlooks the backyard. She has her own closet and her own bathroom. Her brother's room, on the other hand, is fairly small. Though her older brother was given first choice of rooms, he chose the smaller room because it felt cozier. His room has a smaller closet, no private bathroom, and overlooks the front yard.

8. **Spatial**   The walls in Kim's room are bright yellow. She has posters on the walls and striped, yellow curtains.   Her bedspread is yellow and green.

9. **Sequence**   Kim has a system when it comes to cleaning her room. First, she picks up all her toys and puts them away. Then, she makes up her bed. Finally, she dusts and runs the vacuum cleaner.

10 **Cause and Effect**   Kim's dad got offered a new job in a big, new city. It was a very good job with a very good salary, so her family moved over the summer.

Creating a Life Map
for Year-Long Writing Ideas

Sometime at the beginning of the year, (maybe on a Friday when students need a break), hand students a piece of paper and ask them to create a life map. If you provide classroom folders, one of the inside flaps is a great place to draw a life map.

Students begin by writing down where and when they were born. They must draw a symbol which represents their birth in some way. The symbol simply serves as a reminder, so it can be anything (picture of a baby, a state, a building, a flag, etc.)

The students then draw a line in any direction they want to go and write the next event they remember in their lives. They must draw a symbol to reflect something about this event.

The events may include gaining siblings, having an injury, visiting relatives, going on vacation, moving to new locations, gaining or losing pets, etc. Anything that was significant in their lives can be added to the map.

Students must have at least 10 events which lead to their current age.

Next, have students draw a cloud at the top and write what they plan to be doing ten years from now. Make sure they include a visual as representation.

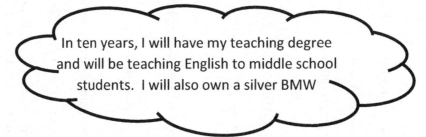

In ten years, I will have my teaching degree and will be teaching English to middle school students. I will also own a silver BMW

You can require students to share some things that they included on their maps as part of a get-to-know-each-other activity.

Throughout the year, when writing essays have students pull out their maps to help them think of ideas.

H.E.L.P. for Writing

H **History**	These examples can include anything from history that you are familiar with. Think about the American Revolution, the Civil War, the Civil Rights Movement, the various presidents, etc., and how they relate to your topic.  
E **Entertainment**	These examples come from current pop culture. Who are the current actors, musicians, sports figures, reality stars, etc., and what do they stand for? Have they done anything controversial or heroic?   
L **Literature**	These examples come from things you have read or movies you have seen. Think of books or stories you have read in the past and why they made an impact on you. What was the author's message?  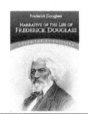 
P **Personal**	These examples come from personal experiences. What are the events in your life that left an impression? Personal experiences usually include the most details because the person writing was there.   

H.E.L.P. for Writing

H **History**	
E **Entertainment**	
L **Literature**	
P **Personal**	

Gilray's Flower-Pot

By J.M. Barrie

I charge Gilray's unreasonableness to his ignoble passion for cigarettes, and the story of his flower-pot has therefore an obvious moral. The want of dignity he displayed about that flower-pot, on his return to London, would have made any one sorry for him. I had my own work to look after, and really could not be tending his chrysanthemum all day. After he came back, however, there was no reasoning with him, and I admit that I never did water his plant, though always intending to do so.

The great mistake was in not leaving the flower-pot in charge of William John. No doubt I readily promised to attend to it, but Gilray deceived me by speaking as if the watering of a plant was the merest pastime. He had to leave London for a short provincial tour, and, as I see now, took advantage of my good nature.

As Gilray had owned his flower-pot for several months, during which time (I take him at his word) he had watered it daily, he must have known he was misleading me. He said that you got into the way of watering a flower-pot regularly just as you wind-up your watch. That certainly is not the case. I always wind up my watch, and I never watered the flower-pot. Of course, if I had been living in Gilray's rooms with the thing always before my eyes I might have done so. I proposed to take it into my chambers at the time, but he would not hear of that. Why? How Gilray came by the chrysanthemum I do not inquire; but whether, in the circumstances, he should not have made a clean breast of it to me is another matter. Undoubtedly it was an unusual thing to put a man to the trouble of watering a chrysanthemum daily without giving him its history. My own belief has always been that he got it in exchange for a pair of boots and his old dressing-gown. He hints that it was a present; but, as one who knows him well, I may say that he is the last person a lady would be likely to give a chrysanthemum to. Besides, if he was so proud of the plant he should have stayed at home and watered it himself.

He says that I never meant to water it, which is not only a mistake, but unkind. My plan was to run downstairs immediately after dinner every evening and give it a thorough watering. One thing or another, however, came in the way. I often remembered about the chrysanthemum while I was in the office; but even Gilray could hardly have expected me to ask leave of absence merely to run home and water his plant. You must draw the line somewhere, even in a government office. When I reached home I was tired, inclined to take things easily, and not at all in a proper condition for watering flower-pots. Then visitors would drop in. I put it to any sensible man or woman, could I have been expected to give up my friends for the sake of a chrysanthemum? Again, it was my custom of an evening, if not disturbed, to retire with my pipe into my cane chair, and there pass the hours communing with great minds, or, when the mood was on me, trifling with a novel. Often when I was in the middle of a chapter Gilray's flower-pot stood up before my eyes crying for water. He does not believe this, but it is the solemn truth. At those moments it was touch and go, whether I watered his chrysanthemum or not. Where I lost myself was in not hurrying to his rooms at once with a tumbler. I said to myself that I would go when I had finished my pipe, but by that time the flower-pot had escaped my memory. This may have been weakness; all I know is that I should have saved myself much annoyance if I had risen and watered the chrysanthemum there and then. But would it not have been rather hard on me to have had to forsake my books for the sake of Gilray's flowers and flower-pots and plants and things? What right has a man to go and make a garden of his chambers?

All the three weeks he was away, Gilray kept pestering me with letters about his chrysanthemum. He seemed to have no faith in me – a detestable thing in a man who calls himself your friend. I had promised to water his flower-pot, and between friends a promise is surely sufficient. It is not so, however, when Gilray is one of them. I soon hated the sight of my name in his handwriting. It was not as if he had said outright that he wrote entirely to know whether I was watering his plant. His references to it were introduced with all the appearance of afterthoughts. Often they took the form of postscripts: "By the way, are you watering my chrysanthemum?" or "The chrysanthemum ought to be a beauty by this time;" or "You must be quite adept now at watering plants." Gilray declares now that, in answer to one of these ingenious epistles, I wrote to him saying that "I had just been watering his chrysanthemum." My belief is that I did no such thing; or, if I did, I meant to water it as soon as I had finished my letter. He has never been able to bring this home to me, he says, because he burned my correspondence. As if a businessman would destroy such a letter. It was yet more annoying when Gilray took to post-cards. To hear the postman's knock and then discover, when you are expecting an important communication, that it is only a post-card about a

flower-pot – that is really too bad. And then I consider that some of the post-cards bordered upon insult. One of them said, "What about chrysanthemum? – reply at once." This was just like Gilray's overbearing way; but I answered politely, and so far as I knew, truthfully, "Chrysanthemum all right."

Knowing there was no explaining things to Gilray, I redoubled my exertions to water his flower-pot as the day for his return drew near. Once, indeed, when I rang for water, I could not for the life of me remember what I wanted it for when it was brought. Had I had any forethought I should have left the tumbler stand just as it was to show it to Gilray on his return. But unfortunately, William John had misunderstood what I wanted the water for and put a decanter down beside it. Another time I was actually on the stairs rushing to Gilray's door, when I met the housekeeper, and, stopping to talk to her, lost my opportunity again. To show how honestly anxious I was to fulfill my promise, I need only add that I was several times awakened in the watches of the night by a haunting consciousness that I had forgotten to water Gilray's flower-pot. On these occasions I spared no trouble to remember again in the morning. I reached out of bed to a chair and turned it upside down, so that the sight of it when I rose might remind me that I had something to do. With the same object I crossed the tongs and poker on the floor. Gilray maintains that instead of playing "fools tricks" like these ("fools's tricks!") I should have got up and gone at once to his rooms with my water-bottle. What? and disturbed my neighbors? Besides, could I reasonably be expected to risk

catching my death of cold for the sake of a wretched chrysanthemum? One reads of men doing such things for young ladies who seek lilies in dangerous ponds or edelweiss on overhanging cliffs. But Gilray was not my sweetheart, nor, I feel certain, any other person's.

I come now to the day prior to Gilray's return. I had just reached the office when I remembered about the chrysanthemum. It was my last chance. If I watered it once I should be in a position to state that, whatever condition it might be in, I had certainly been watering it. I jumped into a hansom, told the cabby to drive to the inn, and twenty minutes afterward had one hand on Gilray's door, while the other held the largest water-can in the house. Opening the door, I rushed in. The can nearly fell from my hand. There was no flower-pot! I rang the bell. "Mr. Gilray's chrysanthemum!" I cried. What do you think William John said? He coolly told me that the plant was dead and had been flung out days ago. I went to the theater that night to keep myself from thinking. All next day I contrived to remain out of Gilray's sight. When we went, he was stiff and polite. He did not say a word about the chrysanthemum for a week, and then it all came out with a rush. I let him talk. With the servants flinging out the flowerpots faster than I could water them, what more could I have done? A coolness between us was inevitable. This I regretted, but my mind was made up on one point: I would never do Gilray a favor again.

Logical Fallacies

When an argument goes wrong, it's because the opponent has committed a *fallacy*. A *fallacy* is an error in logic – a place where someone has made a mistake in his or her thinking. It is using **bad reasoning** to try to prove an argument. These are some of the more common **logical fallacies**.

Ad Hominem – An ad hominem is an attack on the person making the argument rather than the argument itself with the intention of diverting attention and discrediting the argument.

Example: You say that the Earth is round, but you got a D in science last year!

(The fact that the person making the argument received a D in science has nothing to do with the scientific proof that the Earth is round, so this is not a good argument.)

Hasty Generalization – A hasty generalization is when one forms a conclusion from a sample that is either too small or too special to be representative.

Example: Chick-fil-a is definitely the best fast-food place in the world. It is always crowded when I go there.

(The person making the argument hasn't been to all of the fast-food places in the world, and just because this person's Chick-fil-a is always crowded doesn't mean it's the best. This person's experience is far too small to make such a claim.)

Red Herring – A red herring is an attempt to derail an argument or avoid the question by introducing something irrelevant or out of context.

Example: We need to pass a law to end the sale of dogs from breeders. Cats bought from breeders tend to be more difficult to socialize.

(A person is trying to make the argument that people should rescue dogs from the pound rather than buying dogs from breeders. Cats have nothing to do with the argument, so they are irrelevant.)

Straw Man Argument – A straw man argument is changing or exaggerating an opponent's position to make it easier to refute.

Example: My opponent says that we should end world hunger. He obviously doesn't care about all of the homeless people in America.

(The opponent is simply trying to help those who are suffering throughout the world. The other person changes what the opponent is actually saying by claiming that since he wants to help people throughout the world, he doesn't want to help those in his own country.)

Non-Sequitur – A non-sequitur argument is an invalid argument whose conclusion is not supported by its premise.

Example: Sophie drives a car. Sophie must be rich.

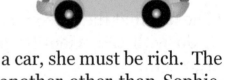

(The person is trying to argue that since Sophie drives a car, she must be rich. The two statements don't have anything to do with one another other than Sophie. Anyone, rich or poor, can drive a car.)

Each of the following types of fallacies comes with an example of a teacher who is trying to get a student to stop using his phone and a student's illogical response.

Ad Hominem

Ad hominem is an insult used as if it were an argument or evidence in support of a conclusion.

Example:

The teacher says, "You do not need your phone in this class, so make sure that it is put away."

The student replies, "You aren't being fair because you come from a time when you didn't have cell phones and don't understand the social importance of them.

The student is insulting the teacher by telling her that she is too old to understand how important cell phones are nowadays. A personal attack is not an argument.

Straw Man

With the strawman argument, someone attacks a position the opponent doesn't really hold.

Example:

Teacher says, "You may not have your phones out in my class."

Student responds, "If we don't have phones, how can our parents get ahold of us in an emergency?"

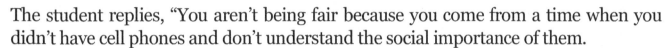

The student is attacking an argument that the teacher did not make. The teacher insists that the phones not be used during class without mentioning whether or not the student should have a phone. The student has a straw man (or weak) argument because he did not address the teacher's original argument.

Slippery Slope

The slippery slope fallacy suggests that unlikely or ridiculous outcomes are likely when there's just not enough evidence to think so.

Example:

The teacher says, "Since you refuse to put your phone away, you need to hand it to me now.

The student responds, "If you take my phone away, my parents won't have any way to get ahold of me. They won't know to pick me up after practice, so I'll end up being stuck here after everyone leaves and probably get kidnapped.

The student's response is extreme in a desperate attempt to keep his phone. He sounds overly dramatic, which makes the argument ineffective.

Red Herring

A red herring fallacy can be difficult to identify because it's not always clear how different topics relate.

Example:

The teacher says, "Stop using your phone and put it away."

The student responds, "I was just looking up what you were saying about writing an essay the other day. Could you explain that again?"

The student is trying to distract the teacher from the original argument. He brings up something not related to what the teacher was saying to try to get her to forget about the phone.

Hasty Generalization

A hasty generalization is when one forms a conclusion from a sample that is either too small or too special to be representative.

Example:

The teacher says, "Stop using your phone and put it away."

The student responds, "Teachers don't understand kids. We all need our phones. Our parents and bosses need to be able to get in touch with us?"

The student is using a hasty generalization that all students have jobs and that all their parents need to be able to reach them immediately. In reality, most students don't have jobs and parents can contact the school if they need to speak to the student.

Non Sequitur

A non-sequitur argument is an invalid argument whose conclusion is not supported by its premise.

Example:

The teacher says, "Stop using your phone and put it away."

The student responds, "I wasn't using it to cheat. I was using it to find out what time the game starts tonight. Besides, everyone else is using their phone."

The student is arguing that since everyone else is using their phone and he wasn't cheating, he should be able to use his. This doesn't have anything to do with the fact that he shouldn't be using his phone in class.

225

Gilray's Flower-Pot
Logical Fallacy Identification Chart

Identify the type of logical fallacy used in each example and explain how the logical fallacy applies to the situation

Text Example	Logical Fallacy	Explanation of Logical Fallacy
Gilray deceived me by speaking as if the watering of a plant was the merest pastime. He had to leave London for a short provincial tour, and, as I see now, took advantage of my good nature.		
He said that you got into the way of watering a flower-pot regularly just as you wind-up your watch. That certainly is not the case. I always wind up my watch, and I never watered the flower-pot.		
Undoubtedly it was an unusual thing to put a man to the trouble of watering a chrysanthemum daily without giving him its history.		
Even Gilray could hardly have expected me to ask leave of absence merely to run home and water his plant. You must draw the line somewhere, even in a government office.		
But would it not have been rather hard on me to have had to forsake my books for the sake of Gilray's flowers and flower-pots and plants and things?		

© 2024 Rohach

227

Gilray's Flower-Pot
Logical Fallacy Identification Chart (cont.)

Identify the type of logical fallacy used in each example and explain how the logical fallacy applies to the situation

Text Example	Logical Fallacy	Explanation of Logical Fallacy
Gilray kept pestering me with letters about his chrysanthemum. He seemed to have no faith in me – a detestable thing in a man who calls himself your friend.		
Had I had any forethought I should have left the tumbler stand just as it was to show it to Gilray on his return. But, unfortunately, William John had misunderstood what I wanted the water for and put a decanter down beside it.		
I should have got up and gone at once to his rooms with my water-bottle. What? and disturbed my neighbors? Besides, could I reasonably be expected to risk catching my death of cold for the sake of a wretched chrysanthemum?		
With the servants flinging out the flower-pots faster than I could water them, what more could I have done?		

Gilray's Flower-Pot

Logical Fallacy Identification Chart **Answers**

Identify the type of logical fallacy used in each example and explain how the logical fallacy applies to the situation

Text Example	Logical Fallacy	Explanation of Logical Fallacy
Gilray deceived me by speaking as if the watering of a plant was the merest pastime. He had to leave London for a short provincial tour, and, as I see now, took advantage of my good nature.	Ad Hominem	The narrator is trying to divert the attention from his own mistakes by insulting and attacking Gilray.
He said that you got into the way of watering a flower-pot regularly just as you wind-up your watch. That certainly is not the case. I always wind up my watch, and I never watered the flower-pot.	Hasty Generalization	The narrator is arguing that the watering of the plant isn't as simple as Gilray implied it was, but his example is too simplistic.
Undoubtedly it was an unusual thing to put a man to the trouble of watering a chrysanthemum daily without giving him its history.	Non Sequitur	The narrator is arguing that part of the reason he didn't succeed in watering the plant was because he didn't know its value, which is invalid.
Even Gilray could hardly have expected me to ask leave of absence merely to run home and water his plant. You must draw the line somewhere, even in a government office.	Red Herring	The narrator is attempting to derail the argument by discussing having to leave work, which was irrelevant.
But would it not have been rather hard on me to have had to forsake my books for the sake of Gilray's flowers and flower-pots and plants and things?	Straw Man	The narrator is changing Gilray's intent by claiming that he shouldn't have to forsake his books to water the chrysanthemum.

Gilray's Flower-Pot
Logical Fallacy Identification Chart Answers cont.

Identify the type of logical fallacy used in each example and explain how the logical fallacy applies to the situation

Text Example	Logical Fallacy	Explanation of Logical Fallacy
Gilray kept pestering me with letters about his chrysanthemum. He seemed to have no faith in me – a detestable thing in a man who calls himself your friend.	Ad Hominem	The narrator insults Gilray to deflect his own responsibility in killing the plant.
Had I had any forethought I should have left the tumbler stand just as it was to show it to Gilray on his return. But, unfortunately, William John had misunderstood what I wanted the water for and put a decanter down beside it.	Red Herring	The narrator is attempting to deflect his responsibility by claiming that he intended to water the plant but William John distracted him.
I should have got up and gone at once to his rooms with my water-bottle. What? and disturbed my neighbors? Besides, could I reasonably be expected to risk catching my death of cold for the sake of a wretched chrysanthemum?	Straw Man	The narrator is attempting to claim that Gilray expected him to disturb the neighbors or risk his life when that isn't at all what Gilray wanted from him.
With the servants flinging out the flower-pots faster than I could water them, what more could I have done?	Red Herring	The narrator is avoiding the argument by claiming that it was the servant's fault for removing the plant too soon, which is irrelevant.

230

Gilray's Flower-Pot
Vocabulary in Context Definition Chart

Word in Context	What I Think the Word Means	Dictionary Definition
I charge Gilray's unreasonableness to his **ignoble** passion for cigarettes, and the story of his flower-pot has therefore an obvious moral.		
I had my own work to look after, and really could not be tending his **chrysanthemum** all day.		
Again, it was my custom of an evening, if not disturbed, to retire with my pipe into my cane chair, and there pass the hours **communing** with great minds, or, when the mood was on me, trifling with a novel.		
He seemed to have no faith in me – a **detestable** thing in a man who calls himself your friend.		
Often they took the form of **postscripts**: "By the way, are you watering my chrysanthemum?" or "The chrysanthemum ought to be a beauty by this time," or "You must be quite adept now at watering plants."		

© 2024 Rohach

Gilray's Flower-Pot
Vocabulary in Context Definition Chart

Word in Context	What I Think the Word Means	Dictionary Definition
Gilray declares now that, in answer to one of these ingenious **epistles**, I wrote to him saying that "I had just been watering his chrysanthemum."		
Had I had any forethought I should have left the **tumbler** stand just as it was to show it to Gilray on his return.		
But, unfortunately, William John had misunderstood what I wanted the water for and put a **decanter** down beside it.		
One reads of men doing such things for young ladies who seek lilies in dangerous ponds or **edelweiss** on overhanging cliffs.		
All next day I **contrived** to remain out of Gilray's sight.		

Gilray's Flower-Pot
Vocabulary in Context Definition Chart Answers

Word in Context	What I Think the Word Means	Dictionary Definition
I charge Gilray's unreasonableness to his **ignoble** passion for cigarettes, and the story of his flower-pot has therefore an obvious moral.	Answers will vary.	Ignoble means not honorable in character or purpose.
I had my own work to look after, and really could not be tending his **chrysanthemum** all day.	Answers will vary.	A chrysanthemum is a plant of the daisy family with brightly colored ornamental flowers, existing in many cultivated varieties.
Again, it was my custom of an evening, if not disturbed, to retire with my pipe into my cane chair, and there pass the hours **communing** with great minds, or, when the mood was on me, trifling with a novel.	Answers will vary.	Communing is to share one's intimate thoughts or feelings with (someone), especially on a spiritual level.
He seemed to have no faith in me – a **detestable** thing in a man who calls himself your friend.	Answers will vary.	Being detestable is deserving intense dislike.
Often they took the form of **postscripts**: "By the way, are you watering my chrysanthemum?" or "The chrysanthemum ought to be a beauty by this time;" or "You must be quite adept now at watering plants."	Answers will vary.	A postscript is a note or series of notes appended to a completed letter, article, or book.

233

Gilray's Flower-Pot
Vocabulary in Context Definition Chart Answers

Word in Context	What I Think the Word Means	Dictionary Definition
Gilray declares now that, in answer to one of these ingenious **epistles**, I wrote to him saying that "I had just been watering his chrysanthemum."	Answers will vary.	An epistle is a poem or other literary work in the form of a letter or series of letters.
Had I had any forethought I should have left the **tumbler** stand just as it was to show it to Gilray on his return.	Answers will vary.	A tumbler is a drinking glass with straight sides and no handle or stem.
But, unfortunately, William John had misunderstood what I wanted the water for and put a **decanter** down beside it.	Answers will vary.	A decanter is a stoppered glass container into which wine is decanted.
One reads of men doing such things for young ladies who seek lilies in dangerous ponds or **edelweiss** on overhanging cliffs.	Answers will vary.	An edelweiss is a European mountain plant that has woolly white bracts around its small flowers and downy gray-green leaves.
All next day I **contrived** to remain out of Gilray's sight.	Answers will vary.	Contrived means to deliberately create rather than arising naturally or spontaneously.

© 2024 Rohach

Gilray's Flower-Pot
Author's Purpose Questions

1. What would you do if you promised something to a friend and ended up breaking the promise? Evan if it were accidental, would you take responsibility or point out to them what had happened.

2. After reading the first paragraph when the narrator says, "After he came back, however, there was no reasoning with him …," what can the reader infer about the narrator?

3. Why did the narrator say that Gilray had deceived him?

4. What literary device is that author using when the narrator says, "He said that you got into the way of watering a flower-pot regularly just as you wind up your watch," and what is the purpose of it?

5. When the narrator says, "… but even Gilray could hardly have expected me to ask leave of absence merely to run home and water his plant. You must draw the line somewhere, even in a government office," what comment is he making about the government?

6. What literary device is the author using when the narrator says, "Often when I was in the middle of a chapter, Gilray's flower-pot stood up before my eyes crying for water," and what was the purpose of it?

7. What literary device is the author using when the narrator asks, "What right has a man to go and make a garden of his chambers?" and what was the purpose of it?

8. When complaining about Gilray's letters asking about the plant, what is ironic about the narrator's statement, "I had promised to water his flower-pot, and between friends a promise is surely sufficient"?

9. How would you describe the narrator based on his comments throughout the story?

10. From what point of view is this story written? How does this make the story more effective?

1. What would you do if you promised something to a friend and ended up breaking the promise? Even if it were accidental, would you take responsibility or point out to them what had happened?

   Answers will vary.

2. After reading the first paragraph when the narrator says, "After he came back, however, there was no reasoning with him …,"what can the reader infer about the narrator?

   The reader can infer that the narrator is going to make excuses for not taking better care of Gilray's plants.

3. Why did the narrator say that Gilray had deceived him?

   The narrator claims that Gilray implied that it would be easy to regularly water the plant, but the narrator did not find it easy and felt that Gilray had taken advantage of him.

4. What literary device is that author using when the narrator says, "He said that you got into the way of watering a flower-pot regularly just as you wind up your watch," and what is the purpose of it?

   The author is using a simile to show how simple it is to take care of a plant.

5. When the narrator says, "… but even Gilray could hardly have expected me to ask leave of absence merely to run home and water his plant. You must draw the line somewhere, even in a government office," what comment is he making about the government?

   By saying "even in a government office," the narrator is implying that the government is incompetent.

6. What literary device is the author using when the narrator says, "Often when I was in the middle of a chapter, Gilray's flower-pot stood up before my eyes crying for water," and what was the purpose of it?

   The author is using personification to point out the pressing guilt the narrator continued to feel for not taking care of the plant.

7. What literary device is the author using when the narrator asks, "What right has a man to go and make a garden of his chambers?" and what was the purpose of it?

   The author uses a rhetorical question, which doesn't require an answer, to make a negative point about Gilray.

8. When complaining about Gilray's letters asking about the plant, what is ironic about the narrator's statement, "I had promised to water his flower-pot, and between friends a promise is surely sufficient"?

    The statement is ironic because the narrator is admonishing Gilray for not trusting him, but the narrator did not follow through with the promise.

9. How would you describe the narrator based on his comments throughout the story?

    The narrator is selfish, irresponsible, and careless. Rather than admit that he didn't take care of the plant as he had promised, he tried to deflect blame on Gilray.

10. From what point of view is this story written? How does this make the story more effective?

    The story is written from the first-person point of view. This makes the story more effective because the narrator's continual use of excuses make the story more interesting.

Advertising Activity

1. What is the subject of the advertisement?

2. Who is presenting the ad?

3. Who is the audience (target) of the ad? List all of them.

4. What are both the verbal and visual appeals to Ethos (duty, ethics, responsibility)?

5. What are both the verbal and visual appeals to Pathos (passion, emotions)?

6. What are both the verbal and visual appeals to Logos (logic)?

7. What aspect visually captured your attention first?

8. If characters are present, what are they doing? What does their behavior convey?

9. What images are present? Which images dominate? What word could you use to classify or categorize the images that appear in the ad?

10. What colors are used and what effect is created through the selection of those colors? (Consider symbolism) Is there a contrast of light and dark? What effect does the contrast create?

11. Describe the mood created by the ad? Provide the denotation (dictionary meaning) and connotation (what the word makes the reader feel) of any applicable words.

12. Cite verbal and/or visual examples from the ad that support the mood you have identified.

13. What is one way the ad could have been more effective toward the intended audience?

14. Describe what a commercial of this ad would look like.

15. Express the claim that this ad is making in the form of a thesis statement. (Example: Crest is the best toothpaste because it prevents cavities, whitens teeth, and freshens breath.)

Advertising Activity with Rhetoric Activity

In groups of 2 or 3, use your imagination and invent an original product. (It doesn't have to be real.) Create an effective advertisement using various strategies.

(10) _____pts.   Create an original and memorable slogan.

(10) _____pts.   Use ethos, pathos, and logos. (Each example must be separate.)

(10) _____pts.   Use at least 3 additional rhetorical devices. (Each example must be separate.)

(10) _____pts.   Use a colorful visual.

On the Back of the Advertisement

(5) _____pts.   Write the full name of each group member and the date.

(30) _____ pts.   Write each strategy you used and the effect that was created by it.

(5) _____ pts.   Write a thesis statement that expresses the claim which the advertisement is making.

❖ **Each group member must have his own individual copy of this paper to turn in with the advertisement.**

Example 1

Is it better to try new things or stick with things you know are reliable?

It is better to try new things than to stick to things you know are reliable. If you try new foods, you may find that you like something you've never had before. Sometimes you think you don't like something, but you really do. I like to try new foods at restaurants to find things I like. If you don't know whether or not you'll like something, give it a try and you just might find it's the best thing you've ever had.

Read the paragraph.

Underline the thesis statement.

Highlight the reason (example) in pink.

Highlight the details describing the example in yellow.

Is this paragraph convincing? Why or why not?

How could it be improved?

Is there a conclusion and does it connect to the thesis?

Example 2

Is it better to try new things or stick with things you know are reliable?

Trying new things is important, because if you don't you may never discover the best things life has to offer. One of the things you should always try is new food items. When I was a child, my father kept trying to get me to taste guacamole. It looked strange and unappetizing, so I refused to try it. Finally, one day my dad said he would give me money if I tried it, so I did. I ended up loving it and it became my favorite childhood food. I ate it every chance I got. To this day, I still like guacamole. If I hadn't tried it, I never would have known how great it is!

Read the paragraph.

Underline the thesis statement.

Highlight the reason (example) in pink.

Highlight the details describing the example in yellow.

Is this paragraph convincing? Why or why not?

How could it be improved?

Is there a conclusion and does it connect to the thesis?

Example 3

Is it better to try new things or stick with things you know are reliable?

Trying new things is important, because if you don't you may never discover the best things life has to offer. When I was a kid, I didn't like to try new things, especially food. My dad would always try to get me to sample things, but I was afraid my tongue would fall off or something terrible would happen. One day we went to a Mexican food restaurant, and he wanted me to try guacamole. It was green, mushy, and for lack of a better comparison, looked like baby poop. There was no way I was going to try it. My dad finally pulled a crisp $5 bill out. Thinking about how many Richie Rich comic books I could buy with this small fortune, I decided to risk it. I would try the goop. I took a nice, salty chip, dipped it in the slimy, toxic-looking sludge, stuck it in my mouth and chewed as fast as I could. In the moments before I took a drink of my lemonade, I realized that I actually liked the taste. It had a creamy, lemony, unique taste. Instantly it became my favorite food and I ate it as often as I could. To this day, I still like guacamole. Even better, I discovered that it's good for you! If my dad hadn't convinced me to try something new, I never would have known what a great food it is. Sure, depending on the same, old reliable things are great, but if you don't try things you've never had before, you may be missing out on the best thing you've ever had!

Read the paragraph.

Underline the thesis statement.

Highlight the reason (example) in pink.

Highlight the details describing the example in yellow.

Is this paragraph convincing? Why or why not? How could it be improved?

Underline the conclusion. Does it connect to the thesis?

Writing with Details Result Questions

What is the difference between Example 2 and Example 3?

Which one of the three examples is the most interesting? What makes it more interesting than the others?

Why is it important to add details to an essay?

What is a strategy that you can use to help you think of examples for the essay?

Writing with Detail
Group Exercise

1. Have students get in groups of three or four.

2. Give students the following topics:

    - Is it better to have loved and lost or never to have loved at all?
    - Describe the worst day that you ever had.
    - If you could change one thing about your school, what would it be?
    - If you could have one superpower, what would it be and why?
    - If you suddenly inherited a million dollars, what would you do with it and why?

3. Have each person in the group choose a different topic.

4. Give students 5-10 minutes to write a paragraph about their topic.

5. After the time expires, have students pass their paper to the person on their right.

6. Give that person 5-10 minutes to re-write their peer's paragraph adding details.

7. After the time expires, have the students pass the paper they are working on to the person on their right.

8. Continue this process until everyone in the group has written on each topic. Each time a paper is re-written, details must be added.

9. When students are done, have them take turns reading the original paragraph and the one that has been re-written by everyone in the group.

Example 1

Is it better to try new things or stick with things you know are reliable?

It is better to try new things than to stick to things you know are reliable. If you try new foods, you may find that you like something you've never had before. Sometimes you think you don't like something, but you really do. I like to try new foods at restaurants to find things I like. If you don't know whether or not you'll like something, give it a try and you just might find it's the best thing you've ever had.

Read the paragraph.

Underline the thesis statement.

Highlight the reason (example) in pink.

Highlight the details describing the example in yellow.

Is this paragraph convincing? Why or why not?
This paragraph is not convincing because it keeps saying the same thing over and over. It is repetitive without giving much new information.

How could it be improved?
There are no examples or details to prove the person's position. The writer needs to add examples and details.

Is there a conclusion and does it connect to the thesis?
There is a conclusion, but it doesn't refer to the second part of the thesis.

Example 2

Is it better to try new things or stick with things you know are reliable?

<u>Trying new things is important, because if you don't you may never discover the best things life has to offer.</u> One of the things you should always try is new food items. When I was a child, my father kept trying to get me to taste guacamole. It looked strange and unappetizing, so I refused to try it. Finally, one day my dad said he would give me money if I tried it, so I did. I ended up loving it and it became my favorite childhood food. I ate it every chance I got. To this day, I still like guacamole. If I hadn't tried it, I never would have known how great it is!

Read the paragraph.

Underline the thesis statement.

Highlight the reason (example) in pink.

Highlight the details describing the example in yellow.

Is this paragraph convincing? Why or why not? How could it be improved?

This paragraph is somewhat convincing. It has a good introduction and provides an example that makes sense.

How could it be improved?

The example should include more details. The conclusion sounds good but needs to reconnect to the thesis.

Is there a conclusion and does it connect to the thesis?

This example does not have an adequate conclusion. It wraps up the example but doesn't conclude the thesis.

249

Example 3

Is it better to try new things or stick with things you know are reliable?

Trying new things is important, because if you don't you may never discover the best things life has to offer. When I was a kid, I didn't like to try new things, especially food. My dad would always try to get me to sample things, but I was afraid my tongue would fall off or something terrible would happen. One day we went to a Mexican food restaurant, and he wanted me to try guacamole. It was green, mushy, and for lack of a better comparison, looked like baby poop. There was no way I was going to try it. My dad finally pulled a crisp $5 bill out. Thinking about how many Richie Rich comic books I could buy with this small fortune, I decided to risk it. I would try the goop. I took a nice, salty chip, dipped it in the slimy, toxic-looking sludge, stuck it in my mouth and chewed as fast as I could. In the moments before I took a drink of my lemonade, I realized that I actually liked the taste. It had a creamy, lemony, unique taste. Instantly it became my favorite food and I ate it as often as I could. To this day, I still like guacamole. Even better, I discovered that it's good for you! If my dad hadn't convinced me to try something new, I never would have known what a great food it is. Sure, depending on the same, old reliable things are great, but if you don't try things, you've never had before, you may be missing out on the best thing you've ever had!

Read the paragraph.

Underline the thesis statement.

Highlight the reason (example) in pink.

Highlight the details describing the example in yellow.

Is this paragraph convincing? Why or why not? How could it be improved?
This paragraph is very convincing. It has a great specific example with details. The descriptions make it interesting and more believable. If there is room, another example could be added.

Underline the conclusion. Does it connect to the thesis?
This paragraph had a good conclusion because it connected back to the thesis.

Writing with Details Result Question and Answers

What is the difference between Example 2 and Example 3?

Example 2 has a few details which make the paragraph adequate, but not special. Example 3 has several unique details which make it easier to imagine.

Which one of the three examples is the most interesting? What makes it more interesting than the others?

The most interesting is the third example. What makes it interesting are the specific details in it. The writer uses words like "green, mushy, slimy, toxic-looking sludge" to help the reader feel and visual the food and "creamy, lemony" to taste and smell the food. These specific details make the essay much more appealing to the reader.

Why is it important to add details to an essay?

It is important to add details to make it more interesting to the reader and receive a higher score on an assessment.

What is a strategy that you can use to help you think of examples for the essay?

You can use H.E.L.P. to think of specific examples to write about.

Verb Tense Diagnostic Exercise
Excerpt from *Percy Jackson and the Olympians* by Rick Riordan

Complete the passage by filling in the blanks with the past tense of each verb.

There _____ a huge grinding noise under our feet.   Black
                        (is)

smby_____ from the dashboard and the whole bus _____ with a
        (pour)   (is)

smell like rotten eggs.   The driver_____ and _____ the
                                        (curse)   (limp)

Greyhound over to the side of the highway.

After a few minutes clanking around in the engine compartment, the driver

_____ that we'd all have to get off. Grover and I _____ outside
    (announce)   (file)

with everybody else.

We _____ on a stretch of country road – no place you'd notice if you
        (is)

didn't break down there. On our side of the highway _____ nothing but
                                                            (is)

maple trees and litter from passing cars. On the other side, across four lanes of

asphalt shimmering with afternoon heat, _____ an old-fashioned fruit stand.
                                            (is)

Verb Tense Diagnostic Exercise
Excerpt from *Fahrenheit 451* by Ray Bradbury

Complete the passage by filling in the blanks with the past tense of each verb.

And then, Clarisse _____ gone. He didn't know what there was about the
(is)

afternoon, but it _____ not seeing her somewhere in the world. The lawn
(is)

_____ empty, the trees empty, the street empty, and while at first, he did not
(is)

even know he _____ her or was looking for her, the fact was that by the time
(miss)

he _____ the subway, there _____ vague stirrings of dis-ease in him.
(reach)   (is)

Something was the matter, his routine _____ been _____. A simple
(have)   (disturb)

routine, true, _____ in a short few days, and yet ...? He almost
(establish)

_____ back to make the walk again, to give her time to appear. He _____
(turn)   (is)

certain if he _____ the same route, everything would work out fine. But it
(try)

_____ late, and the arrival of his train put a stop to his plan.
(is)

Verb Tense Diagnostic Exercise
Excerpt from *The Book Thief* by Markus Zusak

Complete the passage by filling in the blanks so that the passage reads consistently in the past tense.

Certainly, there _____ sweat, and the wrinkled pants of breath, stretching
          (is)

out in front of her. But she _____ reading.
          (is)

The mayor's wife, having let the girl in for the fourth time, was _____ at
          (sit)

the desk, simply _____ the books. On the second visit, she had
          (watch)

_____ permission for Liesel to pull one out and go through it, which
   (give)

_____ to another and another, until half a dozen books _____ stuck to
  (lead)   (is)

her, either _____ beneath her arm or among the pile that was climbing
       (clutch)

higher in her remaining hand.

On this occasion, Liesel _____ in the cool surrounds of the room, her
          (stand)

stomach _____, but no reaction was forthcoming from the mute, damaged
       (growl)

woman. She was in her bathrobe again, and although she _____ the girl
          (observe)

several times, it was never for very long. She usually _____ more attention
          (pay)

to what was next to her, to something missing. The window was _____
          (open)

wide, a square cool mouth, with occasional gusty surges.

Verb Tense Diagnostic Exercise
Excerpt from *The Giver* by Lois Lowry

Complete the passage by filling in the blanks with the past tense of each verb.

He _____ in a room filled with people, and it _____ warm with
    (is)   (is)

firelight glowing on a hearth. He could see through a window that outside it

_____ night and snowing. There _____ colored lights: red and green and
    (is)   (is)

yellow, twinkling from a tree which _____, oddly, inside the room. On a table,
                                        (is)

lighted candles _____ in a polished golden holder and _____ a soft,
                    (stand)   (cast)

flickering glow. He could smell things cooking, and he _____ soft
                                                            (hear)

laughter. A golden-haired dog _____ sleeping on the floor.
                                    (lie)

On the floor there _____ packages wrapped in brightly colored paper and
                        (is)

tied with gleaming ribbons. As Jonas _____, a small child _____
                                        (watch)   (begin)

to pick up the packages and pass them around the room: to other children, to

adults who _____obviously parents, and to an older, quiet couple, man and
                (are)

woman, who _____ smiling together on a couch.
                (sit)

Verb Tense Diagnostic Exercise
Excerpt from *The Poisonwood Bible* by Barbara Kingsolver

Complete the passage by filling in the blanks with the past tense of each verb.

He _____ the children less and less. He _____ hardly a father
       (notice)   (is)

except in the vocational sense, as a potter with clay to be molded. Their individual

laughter he _____not recognize, nor their anguish. He never _____ how
       (can)   (see)

Adah _____ her own exile; how Rachel _____ dying for the normal life of
     (choose)   (is)

slumber parties and record albums she _____ missing. And poor Leah. Leah
                                        (is)

_____ him like an underpaid waitress hoping for the tip. It _____ my
(follow)   (break)

heart. I _____ her away from him on every pretense I knew. It _____ no
      (send)   (does)

good.

While my husband's intentions crystallized as rock salt, and while I

_____myself with private survival, the Congo _____ behind the
(preoccupy)   (breathe)

curtain of forest, preparing. to roll over us like a river. My soul was _____
                                        (gather)

with sinners and bloody men, and all I _____ thinking of was how to get
                              (is)

Mama Tataba to come back, or what we should have_____ from Georgia. I
                                   (bring)

_____ blinded from the constant looking back: Lot's wife. I only ever
(is)

_____ the gathering clouds.
(see)

SECTION FOUR

CLASSROOM PROCEDURES

"For every minute spent organizing, an hour is earned."

Benjamin Franklin

A Note for New Teachers

First of all, thank you for taking on one of the toughest but most honorable jobs in the world. You will have some rough days, but you will also have memories and relationships that will last a lifetime.

I have put together some of the basic questions that new teachers have and provided my solutions. Unfortunately, these will not work for all students and all situations. Make sure you think ahead and be prepared. The best advice I have is to pick and choose your battles. Don't' let the small issues get to you. Figure out what is most important and make that a priority.

Remember that you are not alone. Everyone teaching has been in the same position that you are currently in.

Hopefully these procedure ideas will help you navigate these first few difficult years until you find what works best for you.

Best Wishes,

Karen Rohach

Procedures for Classroom Management
Things to Think About

1. What will I assign students when they arrive in class (Do Now, Warm-up, etc.)?

2. How will I provide bell-to-bell instruction?

3. How can I keep students from being disruptive?

4. What if I have a few students who are being disruptive?

Procedures for Classroom Management

Possible Suggestions

1. What will I assign students when they arrive in class (Do Now, Warm-up, etc.)?

    - **I always had a warm-up, do-now, etc. every time students entered my class. If you establish expectations from the very beginning and don't give them time to misbehave, they're less likely to give you problems.**

2. How will I provide bell-to-bell instruction?

    - **I learned early on that I needed to create lessons that took longer than expected rather than ending too soon.**
    - **Have an activity on stand-by with enough copies for all students in case you finish the lesson early.**

3. How can I keep students from being disruptive?

    - **The best way to keep my students from being disruptive was by building a relationship with them. The more I got to know them and prove to them that I cared about them, the more they didn't want to disappoint me. Rather than get angry at them, I would let them know that I was disappointed with their behavior.**
    - **Most students act out because they are craving attention.**

4. What if I have a few students who are being disruptive?

    - **If I had a small group of students being disruptive, I would change their seating arrangements. I would spread them out and sit the worst ones close to the front. After you have exhausted all other avenues (one-on-one confrontation, phone call to parents, etc.), contact an administrator.**

Procedure for Room Set Up
Things to Think About

1. Where will I put my desk?

2. How will I arrange the students' desks?

    *   Should I put them in groups, rows, or other ways?

    *   Am I able to walk around the room and be in proximity to all students?

3. Where will I put supplies for students to use (pencil sharpener, paper, etc.)?

Procedure for Room Set Up
Possible Suggestions

1. Where will I put my desk?
   - **This will most likely depend on where your computer has to go.**
   - **Technology will probably dictate where you put things.**
   - **I made sure my computer screen was facing away from the students and that I was facing my students if I was sitting at my desk.**
   - **I also made sure that there was only one opening to get behind my desk and that it wouldn't be too easy for students to get behind it.**

2. How will I arrange the students' desks?
   - **I personally never liked the straight rows, so I would arrange them in different ways including splitting the class in half and facing each other, having half face forward and half sideways, etc.**
   - **If you decide to put them in groups, you might want to start by putting them in rows first and establishing guidelines for the groups to prevent misbehavior.**
   - **Make sure that no matter how the desks are arranged, no student has his back to you.**
   - **Make sure that you can walk throughout the classroom and reach each student regardless of how you arrange your desks.**

3. Where will I put supplies for students to use (pencil sharpener, paper, etc.)?
   - **I always had a place in the front of my room where I put supplies that students would need. This prevented unnecessary disruptions.**

Procedure for Assignments
Things to Think About

1. Where will students turn in assignments?

2. How will you keep them separated by period?

3. Where will you keep graded papers before you return them?

4. How will you return them?

Procedure for Assignments
Possible Suggestions

1. Where will students turn in assignments?
   - **Students need to have a routine and know the expectations of how to turn in their assignments.**
   - **Some teachers have a stack of trays so that each period can turn their papers in the designated tray.**
   - **I was always worried that students would take each other's papers to copy, so I had one tray on my desk. At the end of the period, I would collect them, paperclip the stack, and set them aside.**

2. How will you keep them separated by period?
   - **Read the bullets above.**
   - **I made sure I always had a large supply of paperclips, and I kept the papers clipped by periods.**

3. Where will you keep graded papers before you return them?
   - **On my desk, I had one of those descending metal folder holders where I kept a folder for each class period. I would put the graded papers in the proper folder.**

4. How will you return them?
   - **Depending on what the assignment was, I would return it immediately or wait until I had a few graded to return them.**
   - **At the beginning of the year, I would return the papers myself so that I could learn students' names faster.**
   - **After I learned the students' names, I would ask for volunteers to return the papers.**

Procedure for Grading
Things to Think About

Follow the district policy as it applies to grading, late work, etc.

1. How many daily grades am I required to have for students per nine-week or six-week period?

2. How many test grades am I required to have for students per nine-week or six-week period?

3. What will I use for test grades?

4. What are assignments that I can take daily grades on?

5. What is the district policy on accepting late assignments? What is my policy?

Procedure for Grading
Possible Suggestions

Follow the district policy as it applies to grading, late work, etc.

1. How many daily grades am I required to have for students per nine-week or six-week period?

    I took as many daily grades as possible so that they had a better chance of passing.

2. How many test grades am I required to have for students per nine-week or six-week period?

    Make sure you know how many are required and plan ahead. The requirement is usually 3 or 4.

3. What will I use for test grades?

    Check with your team to see if they have a plan for test grades. You will probably test over skills as you teach them. I used test grades, essays, and projects (anything that took more time and effort than a daily grade.)

4. What are assignments that I can take daily grades on?

    I took up students' warm-ups at the end of the week and took a grade on them. I often took up assignments just to make sure that students were following along. I gave them completion grades as a reward for paying attention and learning the material.

5. What is the district policy on accepting late assignments? What is my policy?

    I took off ten points per day for late work. If students refused to do work in class, they received a zero. I had them sign a paper saying that they refused to do the assignment in class so that I would have proof that I made attempts to help them pass.

Procedure for Bathroom Request
Things to Think About

Follow the rules and guidelines according to your school or district.

1.   How often will students be allowed to go to the bathroom?

2.   What kind of hall pass will you use?

3.   How will you keep track of who is out of the room and how long they've been out?

4.   How will you keep track of how often each student is leaving your class?

Procedure for Bathroom Request
Possible Suggestions

Follow the rules and guidelines according to your school and district.

1. How often will students be allowed to go to the bathroom?

    - **Students shouldn't need to go to the bathroom more than once a week unless they have a medical issue.**

    - **Some students will ask to go every day if you let them.**

    - **Be aware that students will use the excuse to go to the bathroom so that they can roam the halls or do things that they shouldn't.**

2. What kind of hall pass will you use?

    I've seen teachers using bright yellow vests, a traffic cone, a wooden plaque, etc. I like to use something they can wear around their neck, similar to an ID badge.

3. How will you keep track of who is out of the room and how long they've been out?

    Some teachers use sign-out sheets. One idea I have (which I can honestly say I have never tried) is to have a whiteboard near the door. Have the students sign the whiteboard along with the time as they leave the classroom. That way you can see at a glance how long the student has been out. The next student will erase the name of the previous one and write his own.

4. How will you keep track of how often each student is leaving your class?

    One thing I've done is to use a seating chart and put a quick checkmark by the student each time he goes to the bathroom.

(This was the one I used. Follow the guidelines of your school.)

Classroom Rules

(Specific class)

(Teacher name)

(Teacher email)

Students are expected to comply with the rules in the student handbook at all times as well as the specific rules listed below:

1. Students are expected to be in their desks, wearing their ID badges, and ready for class when the tardy bell rings.

2. Students are not allowed to bring food or drinks in the classroom at any time.

3. Leave the room as you found it. If you use a book, dictionary, etc., put it back where it belongs and clean up any paper around your desk before you leave the classroom.

4. Passes out of the classroom are for emergencies only. Take care of business on your own time. Make sure you sign out if a restroom break is needed.

5. Students will participate in classroom discussions with maturity. Students will be respectful of their classmates and the teacher at all times. Behavior problems, rude behavior, and excessive distractions will not be tolerated.

Supplies

Students are expected to have a pencil and paper when they come to class.

Grading Policy

Major Grades: Tests, Essays, Projects = 60%

Daily Grades, Quizzes = 40%

Works Cited

Atwood, Margaret, and Robert Weaver. "'Bread.'" *The New Oxford Book of Canadian Short Stories in English*, Oxford University Press, Toronto, 1997.

Bambara, Toni Cade. "'Blues Ain't No Mockin Bird' ." *We Be Word Sorcerers: 25 Stories by Black Americans*, Bantam Books, New York, 1973.

Barden, Thomas E. "'Catch the Moon' by Judith Ortiz Cofer." *Short Stories for Students. Presenting Analysis, Context, and Criticism on Commonly Studied Short Stories*, Gale, a Cengage Company, Farmington Hills, MI, 2018.

Barrie, J. M. "Gilray's Flower-Pot." *Goodreads*, Goodreads, https://www.goodreads.com/book/show/27155089-gilray-s-flower-pot.

Bradbury, Ray. *Ray Bradbury Stories*. Harper Voyager, 2008.

Douglass, Frederick. *Narrative of the Life of Frederick Douglass, an American Slave*. Dover Publications, 1955.

Edwards, Jonathan. "Sinners in the Hands of an Angry God." 8 July 1741, Enfield.

Fish, Charlie. "Death by Scrabble." *Goodreads*, Goodreads, https://www.goodreads.com/book/show/13219119-death-by-scrabble.

Lee, Harper. *To Kill a Mockingbird*. Arrow Books, 2010.

Lincoln, Abraham. "The Gettysburg Address." The Official Dedication of the Soldiers National Cemetery,19 Nov. 1863, Gettysburg.

Longfellow, Henry Wadsworth. "'The Wreck of the Hesperus.'" *Henry Wadsworth Longfellow Poems*.

Rolseth, Harold. "Hey, You Down There!" *Goodreads*, Goodreads, https://www.goodreads.com/book/show/48903748-hey-you-down-there.